The
Book
OF
OMENS

The Book OF OMENS

THE MAGICAL TRUE ADVENTURES OF A SELF-MADE MOVIE STAR

by Jon Jacobs

Spiral Staircase Publishing
MIAMI, FLORIDA

Although the author and publisher have made every effort to ensure the accuracy and completeness of information contained in this book, we assume no responsibility for errors, inaccuracies, omissions, or any inconsistency herein. Any slights of people, places, or organizations are unintentional.

Edited by Laura Schiff
First printing 2003

ISBN 0-9724529-5-8
LCCN 2002112811

ATTENTION CORPORATIONS, UNIVERSITIES, COLLEGES, AND PROFESSIONAL ORGANIZATIONS: Quantity discounts are available on bulk purchases of this book for educational, gift purposes, or as premiums for increasing magazine subscriptions or renewals. Special books or book excerpts can also be created to fit specific needs. For information, please contact Spiral Staircase Publishing, 54 NE 43rd Street, Miami, FL 33137; (305) 576-5957.

TABLE OF CONTENTS

PREFACE ix

CHAPTER 1
Zero Hero 1

CHAPTER 2
The Year of Jon the Actor 37

CHAPTER 3
Countdown 101

CHAPTER 4
In the Can(nes) 137

LUCINDA'S SPELL REVIEWS 153

AFTERWORD 157

*This book is dedicated to
my magical son, Taliesin,
and the love of my life, Tina Leiu.*

My deepest love and appreciation to all those important people whose paths I crossed during this journey, in particular Randala, Craig Robins, Charlotte Lewis, Michael Kastenbaum, Gergely Fonyo, Christina Fulton, Jana Pesek, Sophie Pegrum, Samantha Mehra, Dave Burke, Valerie Chafograck, Greg Gardner, Philippe Dib, David and Tyger Tattersall, Frederick and Joe "The Champion" Chavez—you are all the stars in my Universe. Also to A. A. Attanasio for his novels and his inspiration and grasp of the intangible (Sumner Kagan will always be the Ultimate Zero Hero), and Dr. Bryan Bates for his book on shamanism, *The Way of Wyrd*. To my mom for all her love and the Universe for looking out for us all.

Before you travel this path with me, I want to give you a tiny bit of background, an insight into why I see the world in this particular way. Perhaps it will make the adventure that much more exciting.

In 1976, when I was about ten years old, I was attending a small private school in London. I was something of a quiet dreamer, but I also loved Elvis Presley and I loved to sing his songs. And I was fascinated by the idea of being in movies.

One day a commercial TV director came to the school looking for a boy with big white front teeth for a toothpaste commercial. I did not have those lovely big white front teeth that some kids have and I was not called down from class to meet the director. However, my best friend Freddy Stuart was, and he got the part.

I was thrilled for my friend and at the same time, something was ignited in me. I guess because someone I actually knew was going to be on TV, I realized it must be possible for me too. Soon after, spurred by my newfound obsession, my mother asked me if I would like to go to full-time drama school. I jumped at the opportunity and after a quick audition, I was accepted there. Within moments I was out of my school uniform and dressed in a leather jacket and ripped jeans hanging with the child TV stars of the day. One of my first auditions was for a commercial for Birds Appeal orange juice. A couple of days after the audition, my agent called to say I got the part.

On the day I was due to turn up at Elstree Film Studios to film the commercial, we got a call to say that, in fact, I would first be shooting a test. The director wanted to see whether myself or another boy looked more like the rest of the family he had cast. When I arrived at the studio, I was surprised to discover the other boy was none other than my best friend Freddy Stuart.

Fortunately for me I got the part. But something had happened that day that did not go over my young head. It was a remarkable coincidence I would never forget. It was truly uncanny that it had come down to Freddy and me for that role; the odds against it were enormous. I knew it meant something important. And I took it as a sign that I was going in the right direction. In fact I got very few parts in those early years, but I never forgot that first incident and the pure magic of it gave me the inspiration to carry on.

In 1982, when I was fifteen, I was very much in love with Charlotte Lewis, a beautiful fourteen-year-old model. We had met on a strange night at a friend's house, and although she was not enamored with me, we did become fast friends. Charlotte and I spent a lot of time together and while I was rarely working as an actor her career as a model was exploding.

Charlotte was a little haunted by it all, and she would always say to me, "Jon, what is going to happen to me?" She would ask me this at least twenty times a day. And I would come up with things like, "Maybe you should try acting," and so forth. I even went with her down to the British Equity Office to get her into the actors union. Then one day after watching Roman Polanski's film *Tess* starring Nastassja Kinski, I was struck by the similarity between Charlotte and Nastassja. The next time Charlotte asked, "Jon, what is going to happen to me?" I said, "If you ever meet Roman Polanski, I bet he'd put you in a movie."

Not long after, Charlotte was introduced to Roman Polanski and he cast her as the leading lady in his new film *Pirates*. Once again magic had struck, the coincidence was too great to be anything less than a thunderbolt from the heavens telling me to follow my intuition; I was on the right track.

Once again I watched someone very close me to plucked for stardom, but this time it was for the Big Screen, the movies. If it could happen for her, it could happen for me. It gave me the courage to continue to pursue my dreams for the next few years despite the fact that I still wasn't getting any parts.

Charlotte introduced me to Cris Campion, the young French actor who was to play opposite her, and he and I became great friends. I even spent a week in Tunisia visiting them on the set of *Pirates*. I had a wonderful dinner with Walter Matthau. I was even thrown off the set once for distracting Charlotte. It was incredibly exciting, but I was hungry to get a taste of it myself. When I left Tunisia I vowed to get in shape, because the one thing I could identify that separated myself from Charlotte and Cris is that they were both fantastically fit.

Nothing actually happened for me work-wise in the next couple of years, except that I did indeed lean down dramatically. In 1986 when I was 19, I finally got my first real acting part, a leading role in a fringe theatre production to be directed by James Marcus, who had been one of the gang members in Stanley Kubrick's *A Clockwork Orange.*

After finishing the play, for which I didn't even get mentioned in the reviews, my thirst for a movie was greater than ever. I had never been interested in the theatre and I didn't do another play for fifteen years.

So desperate was I to get a chance to act in a movie, that when I read in the newspaper *The Stage* about a film being made in Greece, I decided to get on a train and go to Greece. I thought I would knock on the door of the production and ask if I could be in it. I had recently won some money on the horses and so I bought my train ticket and set off.

I stopped in Paris and went to the movie theatre to see *Pirates*, which had just opened. Then I headed for the set of director Robert Altman's film *Beyond Therapy*, in which Cris Campion was playing a role. They were filming in the streets outside a restaurant and I sat at a table at a café to watch the action. Suddenly Cris came running out of the restaurant shouting, "Jon! Jon! You got a movie! You got a movie!" I was so embarrassed everyone on the set was staring—I thought he was teasing me.

It turned out that the writer of the play I had done recommended me to a young filmmaker for a role. The filmmaker had called my father, my father called Cris's mother, she had called the set, and Cris, who was thrilled for me, came shouting and screaming to tell me the news. What was so incredible was that there I was visiting the set of Robert Altman, my head filled with dreams and hopes, and the chain of events that would give me my first opportunity to act in a film came to a crescendo at such an auspicious moment! I knew right away that again magic had struck. This was not just a coincidence, it was a sign. It was an *Omen!*

Venice Beach June 12th 2002

Omen:

An occurrence or phenomenon believed to portend the future.

CHAPTER 1

ZERO HERO

12 May 1995,
Venice Beach, California

Just go! So what if everyone looks at you. You don't want to be without tobacco for the whole weekend. Just go to the bank and draw out your last four bucks.

The sun on my back was a pleasant surprise. I guess I was expecting the day to be as depressed as I was. It was three blocks from Valerie's apartment to the bank. The crippled vet pointed to my unzipped fly when I shrugged that I had no change to spare. Usually I like to share my last few cents with the guys on the street; that way it should come back to me. My philosophy is that if all they have to do is stretch out their hands to passersby, then all I have to do is ask the Universe and something will come my way. The only problem is that loose change won't keep a roof over my head. Nor will it afford me the luxury of dating women.

Standing in line at the bank I hoped no one would lean over my shoulder sniggering as I withdrew my last four bucks. I got lucky, it wasn't so difficult after all. A packet of Drum rolling tobacco left me seventy-five cents, add to that another dollar in change jingling at the bottom of my leather money belt and that amounts to a grand total of one dollar and seventy-five cents. The grand sum of my existence. This is where I begin my story: Venice Beach, a dollar seventy-five in cash, a pack of tobacco, fifty rolling papers, and my friend's couch to sleep on 'til the end of the month. A portable computer. An Art Deco chair in burgundy-colored velvet that once belonged to the deceased film star Susan Hayward. An Egyptian tomb figure that is approximately thirty-three hundred years old and is worth about fifteen hundred dollars, but which is not easy to sell in LA. A show print of my first feature film, *The Girl With the Hungry Eyes*, which I wrote and directed and in which I played the role of a serial rapist. And finally, a screenplay called *Lucinda's Spell*, which I wrote and intend to direct and star in when I've raised sufficient cash.

I'm twenty-eight years old. I was born in England and grew up in London. I've been in America since the summer of 1991, struggling to get famous. Two days ago, Valerie, my roommate, went to see a psychic. The woman looked at a photograph of me and told Valerie, in no uncertain terms, that if I didn't start dealing with reality it would be catastrophic for me. Reality scares me. I'm a daydream believer by trade, which means I try to live my dream at all times and avoid menial labour at all costs. But it is possible the psychic is right this time. Especially when you consider my financial situation.

Omen number one: Catastrophe awaits, should I fail to address my present reality in a practical manner. In other words, get a job! Why should I consider the psychic's prediction an Omen? Well, I have just returned from Chicago, where I've been supervising the Midwest premiere of my movie, *The Girl With the Hungry Eyes*. A total of thirty-seven people attended the theatre in eight performances. I lost 650 dollars. I had hoped to make several thousand. Anyway, upon my return to LA, obviously the first thing on my mind is what am I going to do next? How am I going to survive? That's when the psychic's message arrived, so it makes sense that I consider it an Omen and that I interpret it literally.

By the way, this is the point of this book—to analyze the mysterious coincidences that occur daily and try to interpret them correctly. And then to see, with hindsight, if it is actually possible to define these circumstances as omens (messages from the Universe). I would like to end this book upon the completion of my filming my screenplay, *Lucinda's Spell*. So this is our goal from here on—to follow the signs to the fulfillment of this dream.

Omen number two: Unexpected job offer pending. While Valerie was relaying the psychic's message to me, I received a phone call from Cassian Elwes, who exec-produced *The Girl With the Hungry Eyes*. He is trying to raise some money to pay me to give his film *Blue Flame* a limited theatrical release. I hadn't expected to hear from him. So this should also be considered an Omen, especially because the call came while Valerie was telling me her story. The only problem with trying to predict if Cassian will actually come up with the dough is that it means waiting and hoping, as opposed to doing and dealing with reality. So I must say I'm doubtful this Omen is going to feed me next week, and I shall resign myself to following the advice of Omen number one and look for a job. Let's hope I'm wrong.

Omen number one equals deal with reality. Omen number two equals wait for deal to go through. Confusing, isn't it?

13 May 1995

I spent my last buck seventy-five on tea and milk. So here I am, a true zero hero. I also received a phone call from my ex-girlfriend, Christina Fulton, to say that she was sick and wouldn't be able to meet with me today. I should have known better than to contemplate a date with her. For a start, whenever I am with her, I am so overwhelmed with desire and affection that the reality is I'm in cuckoo-land waiting for her to put her four-year-old son to bed so we can be alone. Unfortunately for me, the kid is tireless and I usually fall asleep before he does. Very frustrating.

This ties in beautifully with Omen number one: Deal with reality. The reality is that nothing is real as far as my ex and I are concerned, so I should steer clear. Believe me, it is not as easy as it sounds. I have an extraordinarily strong attraction to this woman. She is also highly talented, funny, and one of the most beautiful women I've ever met. She also played the lead in my movie, *The Girl With the Hungry Eyes*, and will play the lead in *Lucinda's Spell*.

I went on a little reconnaissance to find a job today. I walked up Main Street in Venice, the primary shopping strip, and saw a help-wanted sign in a café, but it was so crowded I decided to wait 'til Monday morning to offer my services. The truth is, I find it a little embarrassing to be asking for a job when there are customers around. Maybe I have an ego problem.

I'm pretty upset about this job business. I'm so eager to be making a movie, but I have zero resources and no one left to turn to for financial support. There's a flower shop looking for a van driver, but I need to give them a DMV printout to show that my license is clean, but even that costs five dollars.

There is a crazy pot smoker who lives in the apartment below me. Often at night he can be heard by everyone on the block sobbing like a child. This morning he was stamping his feet and yelling, "I just made fifty-one thousand dollars! Yeah!" *Fifty-one thousand dollars!* Maybe he'll lend me five bucks to get my DMV printout. No way would I ask him, but it crossed my mind.

I wish I could afford to go rent a movie or, better yet, go to the cinema. Back to reality. What is reality, exactly? I'll have to look in the dictionary, I'm so unfamiliar with it.

Reality: The quality of being real; real existence. Belief in the reality of miracles. That's me! *Belief in the reality of miracles.*

Wow! An Omen right there as I was writing; I look in the dictionary to find the meaning of reality and *belief in the reality of miracles* is used to show *reality* in context....The Omen here is the Universe reminding me that I can make my own reality if I believe.

Okay, so what is my reality? I have no cash or credit or savings. I am presently without the resources to continue to pay rent. I am short of a miracle to finance my movie. My father is in hospital in London, having just suffered a stroke. I am unable to buy an airline ticket and am uncertain of my eligibility to re-enter America should I leave. I also owe money to my friends (investments in my screenplay). I have no girlfriend or steady lover. Nor do I own a car. What I do have is a track record of having made a number of short films, two very low-budget features, ten feature screenplays, some experience distributing my own film, some acting experience, and that's about it. Experience.

I also still have my youth and some very good friends spread across four of the five continents.

All we can do is wait and see what happens next....

15 May 1995

While I was out applying for a job at a café, Mel Brooks took a break from shooting his latest picture and telephoned me, returning a longshot call I made to his offices a few days ago. Unfortunately, I didn't get to speak to him, the irony being that as I attempt to deal with so-called reality, I'm incommunicado when little miracles occur.

Let's see if he calls back.

Also, Cassian Elwes had his assistant James call me to find out what is involved in doing a limited theatrical release. I think they are considering releasing *Blue Flame* themselves, which could mean I will be cut out of the deal. How bizarre life is....

What next?

It appears my father is not making much progress recovering his faculties for speech after his stroke. In addition, his roommate doesn't want him back because my father has run up a seventeen-hundred dollar phone bill calling me in America. And so now it seems my father is not only incapacitated but homeless. It's profoundly disturbing to think about one of your parents sick in hospital and poverty-stricken, and you yourself don't even have the airfare to go and visit.

My mother sent me two hundred dollars. I paid 170 in rent, 13 on food, 3.25 on tobacco…leaving me $13.75 to get my DMV printout and some money to buy coffee when I have my next business meeting.

Mel Brooks called me back! He said we could meet when he finishes his film in July. He also gave me a word of advice: "Don't let anyone second-guess you when it comes to your art." Something to look forward to.

Meanwhile, back at the farm, the latest news is that my film, *The Girl With the Hungry Eyes*, sold 12,500 copies on videotape through Columbia Tri-Star. At 63 dollars per tape, that equals 786,000 dollars. But as I understand it, the film is cross-collateralized with some others that lost money, so I won't see a dime. The budget of the film was 220,000 dollars and it has grossed at least 600,000 dollars in sales to foreign distributors so far.

Oh, the irony of it all.

16 May 1995

I feel better today now that I know my work has generated a profit in America. I feel more legitimate in my insane efforts to find financing for my crazy movies.

17 May 1995

I find I am not inspired to be out aggressively searching for menial employment, despite the fact that I'm still truly broke. Yesterday I had a lunch meeting with this guy Mark Brickman, a talented and energetic man who is busy starting a new entertainment company. I dared not order anything more than coffee. It's terribly awkward being poor. Mark is on his way to England and he proposed giving a copy of my screenplay, *Lucinda's Spell,* to Pink Floyd's manager, who has been known to finance films.

I endeavored to close the deal to distribute Cassian's movie, *Blue Flame,* but it's still not definite. I don't think anything else has occurred in the last few days that portends to the fulfillment of my dreams. Except, perhaps, that Marisa Tomei's manager returned my call to let me know that Marisa will read *Lucinda's Spell* when she returns from Cannes. That is a little miracle itself, considering I could not make her a firm offer.

James, Cassian's assistant who called me to pick my brain about distribution and whom I thought was being given the job I hoped to do, has finally turned out to be an ally in that he works for Merton Shapiro, who is actually going to finance it. And he is now pushing the thing forward in Cassian's absence.

I feel like Valerie is watching me carefully to see if I'm going to go out and get a job. It makes me distinctly uncomfortable. Am I being paranoid, or am I just lazy and developing a guilty conscience? Am I not dealing with my reality by not pounding the streets in search of menial labour?

About a year and a half ago I bet a film producer 100 dollars that *The Girl With the Hungry Eyes* would sell in excess of ten thousand video copies. I wonder if he will pay up?

18 May 1995

Penniless again. Today I walked to Santa Monica on a job hunt. I had an interview at Starbucks, my regular coffee haunt. It's painful to have to face another weekend without any money. A little miracle would be very timely.

I really need to do something about my cash flow, but I don't feel it's my Destiny to start a full-fledged business. My creative dreams are my business. I just need to feed myself in the interim.

21 May 1995

All's quiet on the western front. I still haven't managed to close the deal to distribute Cassian's film. I do have a second interview at Starbucks. I also sent a resume to DreamWorks, Steven Spielberg's new studio. I'm still broke and job hunting.

There seems to be little activity on the part of the Universe with regard to *Lucinda's Spell*, but perhaps I'm wrong. Nothing profoundly unexpected has occurred lately.

23 May 1995

Marcus, a friend from London who has been visiting my father in hospital, called to suggest I return to London to take care of things. I do not feel strongly I should be there, despite the fact I would love to be supportive of my father at this time. I need a clear sign from the Universe to suggest this is the direction I must go. Perhaps if I can't find a job in the next week, I will interpret that as the sign I'm not meant to be in LA.

26 May 1995

I stopped by a bookstore in Santa Monica, but they only pay five dollars an hour, so I didn't push for a job.

My ex called to make arrangements to see me two nights running and flaked on both occasions. Boy, do I set myself up for it. The problem is mine, though, because what happens is that she calls telling me of her troubles, and I cannot resist but offer her comfort. Then she suggests we see each other, and in my mind I start thinking maybe we will get back together, but then she flakes and I just get frustrated. What a stupid vicious circle. The fact that she flakes is a clear sign that she doesn't really care for me, especially since she doesn't even call to cancel. What an idiot I appear on paper.

I had my second interview at Starbucks today. The manager gave me the impression she is keen to hire me. The only difficulty is that the location of the store is at least eight miles from where I live, and there is no direct bus route. I've decided I shall cycle to work, which is a brilliant idea because it will get me exercising out of necessity. And I will be in great shape for my movie when I've raised the money.

Another interesting thing about the manager is that she used to manage the store in Hollywood I used to go to every day with my ex-girlfriend. I remember there was a guy who worked at the store who my ex used to flirt with right in my face. How weird that I may now be doing his job. This coincidence is surely a sign from the Universe. Perhaps it means this job is a dead certainty or could it mean Starbucks is going to be trouble for me?

27 May 1995

I've been watching movies like there is no tomorrow: *Forrest Gump, Quiz Show, Braveheart, Crimson Tide,* and *Ed Wood,* all in two days.

On Tuesday afternoon I will find out if I'm gonna get this coffee shop job. Aside from that, nothing dramatic is in the cards for the weekend.

30 May 1995

I spent the night at my ex-girlfriend's house. I am a fool for love where she is concerned.

I had to go to Starbucks today to fill in some forms. My ex gave me some clothes because all I have is torn jeans and I can't afford to buy any new clothes myself. Fortunately, she wears a lot of oversized men's clothing. So it seems I have the job at Starbucks, which is the little miracle I was asking for and also the first full circle I have experienced since I started writing this journal. Even more amazing when you consider that I must have filled in fifteen applications at various stores, and this is the only one that has turned into anything. I have, I believe, dealt with my reality and hopefully averted any possible catastrophe.

1 June 1995

My ex had a two-hour meeting with Steven Spielberg. He is interested in working with her. He says he's her biggest fan. He has seen her in a *Red Shoe Diaries* episode and he has also seen her in my film *The Girl With the Hungry Eyes*, which he referred to as "the horror flick." If Spielberg actually does something for her, then perhaps I can leverage the financing based on her in the lead.

I received a call this morning to say the contract has been signed for me to distribute Cassian's film, *Blue Flame*. If this goes through, then it will earn me about fifteen hundred dollars, enough to find an apartment and buy a cheap car.

I spoke to my father. He seems very low, but he understands my need to stay in America.

Now I must focus harder on finding the 1.5 million dollars for my movie, *Lucinda's Spell*. Let's see what takes shape. I must work hard to get the script out to as many people as possible before I start working eight hours a day at the coffee shop.

2 June 1995

My ex brought me a bunch of clothes to wear for work. We spent the day browsing antique shops in Santa Monica. I am going to endeavor to restrain my sexual desires and my emotional needs to get a clearer understanding of what our relationship is really about.

4 June 1995

Jana Pesek stopped by today. She designed the artwork for the theatrical release of *The Girl With the Hungry Eyes*. She confessed that she has fantasies of being involved in making *Lucinda's Spell*. I told her I have had similar thoughts, and suddenly we felt very close. She is a very talented individual with whom I hope to continue working. Perhaps we will hear more about her soon.

A woman who recently overcame a heroin addiction watched an unreleased feature film that I starred in called *Welcome Says the Angel*. She said she loved it and that it truly moved her, which is quite a compliment because it is a love story involving a heroin addict and a man (me) who tries to save her. This feedback is an Omen, in that it confirms my belief this film must be put out into the world. There is undoubtedly an audience. Also, it communicates and rings true.

No money yet to distribute Cassian's film. Soon, please!

5 June 1995

A very quiet morning. I don't have any clever moves planned. No check has been issued as yet for me to distribute the *Blue Flame* movie. Tomorrow I start training to work at Starbucks. A little thing occurred this evening that could be construed as an Omen, but if it is a literal Omen, then it will be extraordinary. I was talking to my ex about the difficulty of financing *Lucinda's Spell*, and she joked that maybe I'll meet Steven Spielberg at Starbucks. This has already crossed my mind because he lives in Pacific Palisades, where I'll be working. Then I was talking to Bret Carr, a good friend of mine, and he also suggested maybe I'll meet Spielberg in there. Will I? Is this an Omen or just wishful thinking?

Starbucks! Star. Bucks. Star equals fame. Bucks equals fortune. Fame and fortune!

I once worked in a café in London. It was there that I met Philippe Dib, a young business student who professed to having an interest in filmmaking. Later, due to my encouragement, he quit business school and took film courses at UCLA. I eventually joined him in Hollywood and together we wrote a screenplay called *Welcome Says the Angel*. He raised thirty thousand dollars and directed the film, while I played the lead role.

It was my first starring role in a feature film. In fact, it was the first feature film I ever even spoke in. Starring in movies has always been my biggest ambition and my greatest passion.

Coffee shops are lucky for me. That in itself is another Omen!

6 June 1995

Valerie lent me twenty dollars to get buses to Beverly Hills for my job training. I bought some tobacco at the little convenience store across from where I live and I noticed one of the headlines on the front cover of the entertainment trade paper *Daily Variety*. "Jacobs Inks Deal With DreamWorks." I had to read it twice to make sure it wasn't me. DreamWorks is Spielberg's new company. Another sign, or am I getting delusions of grandeur?

12 and 13 June 1995

Back to reality. I borrowed a friend's bicycle and cycled to work at Starbucks—an enjoyable exercise. Besides that, all has been very quiet. Except that Melissa, who is a good friend of my ex and who is also Jim Carrey's ex-wife, paid for a few photocopies of *Lucinda's Spell* and is going to attempt to get Roseanne Barr to consider playing one of the supporting roles.

My short films arrived by mail from London, so I can now set up a meeting with Miramax Films. Over the last few days, things have been interesting for me, but nothing has occurred that I can interpret as a signpost guiding me towards my Destiny.

In fact, I feel depressed.

14 June 1995

It was a good thing Valerie's psychic gave her the message I should deal with reality or else a catastrophe would occur, because it is only my job at Starbucks that is sustaining my mission to fulfill myself.

The film distribution deal has been held up because of some political issue between the director and financier.

I find I am reluctant at this moment to pursue name actresses to star in my movie, because my first choice for the role is still my ex, and I want to wait as long as possible to see if this Spielberg connection will help. However, my ex is unquestionably a handful.

I feel the emphasis of my personal growth at this time lies in the direction of communication and relations with women, because that is unquestionably one of my weakest areas.

17 June 1995

Something funny just occurred to me. The fact that Jim Carrey's ex-wife Melissa paid for the printing of a few of my scripts means that it was, in fact, probably paid for with money earned by Jim Carrey. (The biggest money spinner in Hollywood today—perhaps some of his fortune will rub off on me. He just did a deal with Columbia pictures. His fee is twenty million dollars.) In fact, Jim Carrey and I have a number of strange things in common. Do they constitute an Omen, I wonder?

1. My middle name is Carey, and my stage name used to be Jon Carey.

2. Jim and I met once, and he immediately expressed his frustration and desire to be in movies. This was before *Ace Ventura*.

3. The opening scene in *Ace Ventura* takes place in the Tides Hotel in Miami Beach. The opening scene in my film *The Girl With the Hungry Eyes* was also shot in the Tides Hotel in Miami Beach. I shot my movie first.

4. Peter Greene, who played opposite Carrey in *The Mask,* has agreed to star opposite me in *Lucinda's Spell.*

My interpretation of this strange synchronicity is that my own path will continue to parallel Carrey's in unusual ways. Hopefully, in relation to the degree of success!

I was just struck by another Omen. I went to the corner store to get change for the laundry and I glanced at a copy of *The Hollywood Reporter*. On the front page was a story of an independent film that will star Peter Greene and Tim Roth, to be directed by a guy called Buddy Giovanazzio. This strikes me because Peter Greene has agreed to be in my film, Tim Roth read the script but turned it down, and Giovanazzio's brother created the underscore for *The Girl With the Hungry Eyes*. So I guess this is another sign of good things to come.

Meanwhile, Valerie is very frustrated because she has been advancing me money for the rent and groceries and now she has left herself broke. Unfortunately, despite my job, it will be at least six weeks before I can catch up with what I owe her. The only way to catch up quickly is to borrow money from my mother or sell my computer. I'm sick of borrowing money from my mother, so it looks like it will have to be the computer that goes first. Oh well.

19 June 1995

It's now Monday. I've been working at Starbucks all weekend. I borrowed a friend's car and got a ticket. That is an Omen suggesting I should cycle to work as often as possible.

On Saturday I met three different women named Anna, one of whom I found very attractive. This is an Omen, but what does it mean? (Anna is the name of the girl I play opposite in my first feature *Welcome Says the Angel*.)

I sold my Egyptian statue for 650 dollars to pay off Valerie and leave me some change. Next month's rent should be covered by my paycheck.

Today I'm racking my brains trying to figure out a way to move things forward on my movie. Unfortunately things seem a little slow. I would love to make a breakthrough somewhere, somehow.

23 June 1995

I have accomplished little in the last few days. I'm reduced to seeing my future in the smallest of signs. In *The Hollywood Reporter*, I read that a new company established by Miramax has been named Excalibur, which obviously ties into Merlin, who is a character in my screenplay *Lucinda's Spell*. The same day I read about this, I drove past an LA taxi from a company called Excalibur Cabs. Later in the evening, a friend asked me to pick a tarot card and I pulled the ace of swords. Does this mean that I will, in fact, do a deal with Miramax through this new company, or is it just a sign to remain confident? I do remain confident, but I must do more.

I spent a hundred dollars and joined a gym, leaving myself short of cash. Then I got two parking tickets. I take this as a sign to cycle to work more regularly.

The main issue in my life at the moment is to stop nurturing my emotional attachment to my ex-girlfriend. Nothing seems to be developing between us and perhaps I am causing myself to be closed to new opportunities regarding other women. However, I feel our friendship has found firmer ground at least, and I do not feel the need to banish her from my life—only to stop myself from hoping, wishing for more.

27 June 1995

The Omens continue to flow. To begin with, I finally received the check to finance distribution of the film *Blue Flame*. I will earn fifteen hundred dollars from this, enough to move into my own place and buy a cheap car.

Also, as I was driving in a friend's car yesterday, I was admiring a beautiful vintage car when I noticed it was called Excalibur. Then, farther down the road, I noticed a big billboard advertising the Excalibur Hotel in Vegas. More signs to pursue doing a deal with Miramax's new outlet, Excalibur Films.

28 June 1995

A quiet day. I saw *The Good, the Bad and the Ugly* on the big screen. I received an advance copy of the magazine *Imagi-Movies*, which featured a great review and a two-page color spread on my film *The Girl With the Hungry Eyes*.

8 July 1995

I've been in such an intense swirl for the last two weeks I have not had time to record the details, so I shall attempt to bring things up to date and recall the little significant points.

I am now sitting at my desk in my new apartment. I received fifteen hundred dollars as my fee for distributing Cassian's film *Blue Flame.* I have a hundred remaining to buy a bicycle to get to work.

So I now have an apartment, a phone (in Valerie's name), a desk, and two jobs. With regard to *Lucinda's Spell*, Cassian, who is the head of the independent feature department at the William Morris Agency, has promised to set up a meeting with a company called Kushner-Locke, with a view to financing the film for approximately five hundred thousand dollars. He also proposed to have me read a thriller script to consider me as the director.

The Excalibur theme continues to reoccur, but I have yet to get the meeting going at Miramax Films.

While working at Starbucks, a woman approached me while I was behind the bar. She whispered, "Jon, is that you?" I didn't recognize her until she told me her name. It was my old acting agent from London. She then gave me her telephone number, but it appears it was the wrong number…?

My great friend Randala, the poet, returned from London. She said it was pretty miserable there. I received a telephone call from an Irish actor, Chris Byrne, who was referred to me by Greg Gardner, the publicist at Laemmle's Theatres, where I premiered *The Girl With the Hungry Eyes.* Greg and I get on really well and he's been very helpful to me, so I assume this guy must be interesting. (Chris Byrne introduced me to Sophie Pegrum in October 1997. Sophie wrote and directed *Dogstar*, a movie you will read about later.) We have arranged to meet on Tuesday.

My ex's brother and his wife were in town. She told me they believe she should marry me. She says she's thinking about it. Meanwhile, I haven't heard from her for a week.

I noticed there are black rings under my eyes. I don't think I've been getting enough sleep since I started working at Starbucks.

I submitted my short films that I made eight years ago to the American Cinemateque to be considered as part of the summer film program that will play at the Directors Guild of America.

I feel good but tired. I must now find the energy to start preparing the press release and kit for *Blue Flame,* especially since I already spent my fee in less than a week.

9 July 1995

Nerves under my left eye flutter with tiredness or stress. It's not that I am under terrible pressure, just that I guess I'm used to getting more sleep.

This morning I served a coffee to actor Ray Liotta. It was on my mind to mention a script that Michael Kastenbaum, my longtime friend and producing partner, has developed but the timing felt off. Later in the day I met Jude, a woman who used to be the assistant of Moshe Diamant. Moshe, a producer with whom Michael and I both worked, produced *Time Cop* and other Jean-Claude Van Damme movies. Jude is now working with the director of *The Mask,* who has a three-picture deal with Warner Brothers. Now that I think about it, this is another Peter Greene connection, another Jim Carrey link. I shall pursue this.

I'm going to bed now. It is eleven and my alarm is set for six in the morning. My Starbucks shift begins at seven-thirty.

10 July 1995

Joelle, my old acting agent from London, came into Starbucks again. She insisted that the telephone number she gave me was correct. I'll see; however, I'm not sure I like the vibe between us.

I managed to arrange a screening for Jeff Kurz at Miramax, despite my feeling that I had burdened him with my insistence that he see my short films. When I called his office, I spoke to his assistant, and he immediately said there was a good time this week—and that was that. *Purrrrfect!*

I must write to my father who remains in hospital. I cry after I speak with him. It makes me so sad to feel his predicament.

It is now nine-thirty P.M. and I'm ready for bed.

17 July 1995

Once again, I have to summarize the last couple of days because I'm usually exhausted at night after my Starbucks shifts.

I met with the Irish actor Chris Byrne, and he proposed that we set up a distribution company to fill a gap that exists in the market. It seems he has spent some time hanging out at Laemmle's Theatres, getting a grasp of the business. I am going to follow through with this because, as it is, I am supplementing my income by distributing. Why not capitalize on this further?

Jeff Kurz at Miramax screened my short film. I haven't spoken to him yet, but the owner of the screening room was very impressed.

I received word from the American Cinemateque that they are interested in screening *Sleepwalker,* one of my short films, as part of their summer program. The funny thing about this is that it was made primarily as a trailer (teaser) to find investment for the feature-length version. It will be very funny to me if I receive some recognition for it. Although, now that I think about it, I was considering submitting it to Cannes because I did want it to feel like a short film.

I received a call from Ferdy Mayne, an old actor whom I have cast in the role of Merlin in *Lucinda's Spell.* He is setting up a meeting with the daughter of Robert Shaw (who played Quint, the captain in *Jaws).* It seems she is interested in producing.

As far as the Omens go, I read in *The Hollywood Reporter* that Quentin Tarantino has been given a distribution company by Miramax. Perhaps that is a sign distribution is a good sideline for young film auteurs these days.

Cassian spoke with Michael Kastenbaum, my longtime friend who produced a couple of my short films and also *Welcome Says the Angel* and *Girl with the Hungry Eyes.* First Cassian complained about trying to finance *Lucinda's Spell* with me in the lead role, and then he went on to ask Michael if we could make it for two hundred thousand dollars. Michael told him to just get the money and *then* talk.

I met with Chris Byrne. We drew up an agreement for our distribution company. I'm going to call it Silver

Shadow Pictures. We also came up with a good idea for a film. It's quite unusual that one finds oneself entering into a partnership with a guy you've met but once. An interesting situation, I think.

20 July 1995

I'm in the middle of my second day off work at Starbucks. I bought a bicycle for 180 dollars, leaving me very close to the bone when it comes to paying the rent.

I talked with Jeff Kurz from Miramax. He isn't clear as to how interested he is, but he asked if he could speak to my cinematographer. Then he changed his mind and said that he wants to talk to Michael Kastenbaum who is going to produce the film. Jeff then said he will talk to me soon. I wonder.

The poster for *Blue Flame* is looking good, but I find my energy is low with regard to working on the press package, etc. Silver Shadow Pictures is now in existence, so I'm now officially a distributor. Besides that, the Omens are really not apparent to me of late.

My romantic life is at a standstill.

23 July 1995

It's five P.M. I've just returned from my day's work at Starbucks and I'm now awaiting a call from my ex, who asked me for a date when I called her on Thursday. Unfortunately, because she has flaked so many times this year, I'm a little nervous she is going to cancel and I will find myself disappointed.

I feel as though things are under control with regard to *Blue Flame*. The press release will go out this week and I will probably finish the press kits this week, too.

I feel good in general, so now it would be nice if something solid could actually happen with regard to the financing of *Lucinda's Spell*. I know that if I can raise the million and a half that I'm thinking of, I can make an incredible film.

At least things have progressed from the zero hero stage, which was not so long ago.

I have been cycling to work for the last three days on my new used bike. I'm getting fitter and I'm able to get up to the top of Temescal Canyon without stopping.

My ex and I spent the evening together, but unfortunately, her son wouldn't go to sleep, so we could not be alone.

24 and 25 July 1995

I worked each day at Starbucks, and each night my ex's son was sick, so we could not meet.

27 July 1995

Yesterday I had a meeting with a woman, Deborah Shaw, who runs a film production company with her husband Evzen Kolar. It appears they might be interested in helping to put *Lucinda's Spell* together. The meeting was arranged by Ferdy Mayne, the seventy-year-old actor I have cast in the role of Merlin. The magical aspect of this meeting is that Ferdy has worked with Roman Polanski on two films. In *The Fearless Vampire Killers,* he played the count, and he also appeared as the uncle of Charlotte Lewis, in Polanski's film *Pirates*. Because of this connection with Polanski, perhaps the Ferdy Mayne meeting will lead to something. (I mentioned to Deborah that I was working at the

Starbucks in Pacific Palisades. It appears that it is her local coffee stop.) Omens?

I spent last night with my ex on intimate terms. The bond between us is very strong. The question remains: Will we be able to forge our love into a relationship that is healthy and constructive?

31 July 1995

All is quiet with regard to new contacts concerning *Lucinda's Spell*. I called Mel Brooks today and left a message. I paid August's rent, and I'm gearing towards the *Blue Flame* press screening on Friday. Now Silver Shadow Pictures just needs some action.

1 August 1995

The artwork for Silver Shadow Pictures is going well. I dropped in a videotape of my first feature, *Welcome Says the Angel,* to Blair Murphy. He has distributed his own film on video and now has a label. We are considering joining forces. Blair's office is surrounded by Egyptian artifacts. Perhaps this is an Omen of good fortune in our endeavors together.

All is quiet with regard to the opposite sex.

6 August 1995

Today I'm meeting with Prince Stash Kowoloski: filmmaker, jetsetter, musician, and son of the famous surrealist Balthus. Stash is interested in releasing his feature film, *The Shining Blood,* through Silver Shadow Pictures. Stash is also friendly with Greg Gardner, my good friend at Laemmle's Theatres. Stash also spent time at Paul McCartney's house in London on Cavendish Avenue, which is the street where I grew up. Stash had also seen the film *Welcome Says the Angel,* which I starred in, because he was given it by Michael and Seth Kastenbaum. This, I believe, constitutes a series of cool coincidences that I must construe as a positive Omen. My goal here is to release Stash's film successfully and on the back of it, get the financing to release *Welcome Says the Angel.*

On Friday, I held a press screening for *Blue Flame,* and we had a full turnout from the press. This is a good start for my distribution enterprise.

My ex didn't return many of my calls this week, which sent me into somewhat of a negative spiral. I realize I have much work to do on myself, and I must maintain my distance with her.

I met with Deborah Shaw and her husband on Friday and we talked further of *Lucinda's Spell,* but they will be busy for the next few weeks.

Jeff Kurz at Miramax has not made contact since our last conversation.

9 August 1995

On my way to drop off a newspaper ad to the Laemmle's Theatre chain, I bumped into Chris, my new business partner. How interesting.

I talked to Jeff Kurz of Miramax. He doesn't feel that Miramax would help to produce *Lucinda's Spell.* Distribute, maybe.

15 August 1995

Brenna, a very lovely young actress/singer who works at Starbucks with me, has been involved in an interesting series of Omens. First, she invited me to a party that took place at Paramount Ranch, where I had once worked as an extra on *Mad at the Moon*, a western starring Mary Stuart Masterson that was produced by my friend Michael Kastenbaum. Then we discovered she is in the same acting class as my distribution partner Chris. Then she introduced me to her friend Adam, who is good friends with Cassian's assistant, and then I bumped into Adam at Powerhouse Gym. It turns out he is based at a production company called Stone Circle Films, which is located in the same building as another company called Merlin Productions. My screenplay *Lucinda's Spell* begins with the great-grandson of Merlin performing magic in a stone circle. In addition, I have walked past this building many times and wondered about Stone Circle Films.

I've been busy establishing my distribution company Silver Shadow Pictures. I have not called my ex in ten days!

19 August 1995

I met a pretty girl, Dawn, three times in twenty-four hours. Each time I saw her, she smiled very sweetly. I sent her three roses.

I am working towards the theatrical premiere of the movie I starred in, *Welcome Says the Angel*.

26 August 1995

Just got home from Starbucks. Not much doing, no interesting messages on my machine.

I met with Dawn. I didn't feel any love vibes from her, but her roommate Monica was pretty flirtatious.

The *Blue Flame* project is over. Nothing seems to be happening at the moment with *Lucinda's Spell*. My new focus is definitely the theatrical release of *Welcome Says the Angel*.

29 August 1995

Yesterday I spent two hundred dollars, which was left over from the *Blue Flame* budget, on letterset and cell for *Welcome Says the Angel*. So it is at least now underway. I decided to resist my impulses to phone my ex today, and I feel better for it.

Nothing seems to have come from meeting Dawn, and no additional Omens have struck me of late. I am currently awaiting the arrival of a lover I met at Starbucks. Dogs are howling outside my widow.

3 December 1995

Excuse the gap, but I guess Starbucks got the better of me. However, I'm back with plenty of stories to tell.

To start with, Philippe, the director of *Welcome Says the Angel*, sent me five thousand dollars in September to complete postproduction of the film and prepare the theatrical release. Most of the work is now done, and the premiere is set for Valentine's weekend at the Laemmle Sunset 5, exactly a year since I opened *The Girl With the Hungry Eyes* at the same theatre.

My friend Randala came to stay with me and finished her book of poems while she was here. She is leaving at the end of the month. My first short film was based on one of her poems and landed me at the Cannes Film Festival, so I'm very glad to have been here for her while she needed somewhere to finish her book.

Adam, the young actor I met through Brenna, the girl at Starbucks, asked me to direct him in a showcase performance of a scene from *Beyond Therapy*, which I did. It went well. (I was on the set of Robert Altman's film version of *Beyond Therapy* many years ago when I received a phone call urging me to return to London to play a role in a short film that was essentially the first lead in a film I ever had.) Also, Adam is now dating the girl Dawn, who I met three times in a row and sent three roses. Their meeting had nothing to do with me. Adam and I have decided to make a film together, which we shall write soon.

While behind the counter at Starbucks a few weeks ago, I was offered a job driving people to and from the airport. I accepted it because it pays twelve dollars an hour (double Starbucks). So I no longer work at Starbucks.

I have had a wonderful run on lovers lately and have been having a ball. I met a lovely girl, Andrea, who is very *kewl*, a real California dream. Her half-brother Cliff is the illegitimate son of the Doors' Jim Morrison.

My ex says she is emotional about our relationship— or lack of one. I don't know where that leaves us, but, as usual, I'm open to working things out between us, even though I'm now a man with many lovers.

Many other things have happened over the last few months, but I will have to refer to them as they affect the present. Starbucks was a good experience, particularly because I cycled sixteen miles per day, and also because I rejoined the human race and found myself to be quite capable of sustaining a real job, even though sometimes I was so off-the-wall the customers must have thought I was a character out of a Monty Python film. I think the Pacific Palisades will miss me.

Also, I was interviewed by *E! News* on E! Entertainment Television. They did a special on cult movies, showing clips from *The Rocky Horror Picture Show*, *Eraserhead*, and my film, *The Girl With the Hungry Eyes*. They also interviewed John Waters and David Lynch. Unfortunately, I missed it when it was aired, but as I understand it, the thrust of the story was, "Is *The Girl With the Hungry Eyes* the next big cult film?"

My dad is doing a bit better lately. I'm going to go see him in March or April, I think.

Anyway, that brings things fairly up to date. I have thirty-two hundred dollars in the bank and the Hollywood premiere of my first leading role in a feature film set for Valentine's weekend. Maybe I'll get some interesting reviews on my acting. All these wonderful advents in my life hopefully will bring me closer to getting the financing for *Lucinda's Spell*.

4 December 1995

I drove a couple of Japanese businessmen to the airport and a bunch of eleven-year-old girls to and from school. I earned sixty-five dollars for my trouble.

7 December 1995

Yesterday, I heard that I was on TV in England on Channel 4, on a show called *Hollywood Report*. They did a special on vampire movies.

My emotional ex-girlfriend hasn't called me all week. I guess she's feeling better and less inclined to get involved with me. I have not called her because I find that I'm really only interested in what comes from her unprovoked.

Randala and I are getting on well. I drove her around Hollywood today so she could drop off tapes to various record producers. I'm certain she will, at some point, be recognized as the most important poet of our generation and amongst the most important of all time.

8 December 1995

Welcome Says the Angel was not selected for competition at the Slamdance Film Festival at Park City, Utah. What does this mean? The film has not been selected for competition anywhere. I must focus heavily on the Los Angeles premiere, the only hope for exposure. The organizer of the festival, Jon Fitzgerald, is lobbying to give the film a special screening. We will see. Whatever happens, I will turn all setbacks to my advantage.

10 December 1995

I'm pissed with the weight I feel on my shoulders when contemplating the emotions of my ex-girlfriend that remain unexpressed in a tangible, physical, sacrificial form. It distracts me from my lovers and the possibility of any depth to our relations.

Besides this, I'm also juggling the release of *Welcome Says the Angel*, my driving job, and everything else in life. I feel I'm not managing my time properly and my apartment is dirty.

My mom Jacky White, Miss UK 1962. She should have been a movie star!

One of my first TV commercials at age 11, "Batchelors Square Shape Soup." They built me a square head.

Me, age 13, third from the left with some of the characters from Sylvia Young's Theatre School.

Cris Campion and I in Versailles, France. A photo taken by his mom.

Another photo taken in France the same day I got my first film role.

33 Clubhouse Avenue, Venice, California. "Where the adventure begins!"

Me with my 3000-year-old ancient Egyptian statue, which I sacrificed to pay the rent.

My friend and room mate Valerie Chafograck whose visit to the psychic triggered the first omen.

My great friend Randala, poet, filmmaker, and sometime room mate! (Photo taken outside 33 Clubhouse.)

CHAPTER 2

THE YEAR OF JON THE ACTOR

**16 January 1996,
Venice Beach, California**

It is a terrible crime that I have not recorded each day the variety of incidents that have occurred; however I shall endeavor to catch up.

I vegetated over Christmas. I felt so lazy and lethargic, so much so that I laid off all my lovers. However, the year began well and I earned 150 dollars on January 1, driving a family back and forth to the Rose Bowl.

At the end of the first week, things really started to happen. I picked up a copy of the tape that was broadcast on *E! News*. To my absolute glee, I discovered I had not only been interviewed but had become the subject of a cleverly constructed breaking story. The heavens truly smiled upon me. *E! News* broadcast me as the next cult director to cross into big box office, in the fashion of David Lynch and John Waters. This piece works like the ultimate promo, far beyond my hopes.

On Monday, January 8, I was told the magazine *Cinefantastique* has chosen *The Girl With the Hungry Eyes* as the Best Horror Film of 1995.

On Friday, January 12, I had the first press screening for *Welcome Says the Angel*, a movie I co-wrote and star in and which I have long been praying will give me credibility as an actor. The screening went well. The audience, which included *The LA Times, LA Weekly, LA Village View,* and *The LA Reader,* appeared to tap in to the few moments of subtle humor, which appeared to me as an indication of their involvement with the story.

Since then, I have written new press releases, including the news of my recent recognition, in an attempt to get more press and to start building upon this idea of cult filmmaker. I have felt a little over-hyped, yet I feel like I must seize the moment and get stuff written on me to help cement my presence in America. Then today, whilst in the midst of sending out new press materials, I heard that Sean Smith, the reviewer for *LA Village View,* was very enthusiastic about the film and was looking for more info. I have taken this as a sign to continue my promotional frenzy.

Other good things that have happened in the last month include a twenty-minute conversation with Mel Brooks, in which I was able to pep talk him about his new movie, which did not open well. We are due to meet in March.

Things are feeling very positive.

21 January 1996

I talked to Thomas Harris, who is the programmer at the Los Angeles Independent Film Festival. He said he loved *Welcome Says the Angel* and would spread the word while at Sundance. He also confirmed that Sean Smith of the *Village View* loved the film. I feel that I must still continue to *push, push, push* and to exploit the *E! News* story. I must motivate myself strongly.

Randala returned to England, so I now have space in which I should really start writing. But I must confess to feeling somewhat lethargic when it comes to writing. However, it will be done.

Aside from this, I don't think there have been any more profound Omens. The emphasis for me right now is to be consistent and insistent.

My instincts told me to call this year "the Year of Jon the Actor"; perhaps that is an Omen in itself.

23 January 1996

There are so many signs that seem to indicate my being propelled into the major league that it is quite overwhelming.

Ever hear the song *John Jacob Jingleheimer Schmidt?* His name is my name too! "Whenever we go out/The people always shout/There goes John Jacob Jingleheimer Schmidt!" That is not just an Omen, it is prophetic. Americans have been prepared for my arrival for a long time, it seems.

29 January 1996

I picked up a couple from the airport yesterday, and they asked what had brought me to America. I told them filmmaking. As the conversation went further, they told me their daughter had made a film. It then unfolded that it was produced by Cassian Elwes, who also produced my film, and that it was shot by Gary Tieche, who also shot my film. The woman then relayed a story about how John Landis had once picked them up from the airport when he was a young struggling filmmaker.

Ten days ago, while at Bokaos, my friend Fredrick (a friend with whom I have much in common, including women) introduced me to two producers, Richard Gitlin and Mimi Polk. Richard works at Warner Records and his wife Mimi produced Ridley Scott's latest film, *White Squall*. Richard is interested in seeing short films, so I shall send him a copy of mine. There are potentially many magical Omens that produced this seemingly chance meeting, so I shall endeavor to pursue it. (Although I have not yet met Mimi again, I shot *The Wooden Gun* on her father's ranch in Wyoming in November 1996. Her brother, Steve Polk, costarred.)

I keep noticing clips of Mel Brooks' vampire flick on TV at the airport, so I should go see this film in order to have some common ground with Mel if we do, in fact, meet. In addition, is it not perhaps an Omen that we both made comedic vampire flicks...?

31 January 1996

Today is one of the days I've been waiting for. This last week, I have been walking into my apartment after every little excursion, checking the messages on my machine to see if any more news had filtered back from the critics. Well, today it happened. Greg Gardner called and said that Kevin Thomas of *The LA Times* was raving after seeing the film, calling it stunning and using so many adjectives Greg could not even remember them. Kevin had immediately gone on to say that he was passing it on to someone called Christina (Omen—name of my ex) to see if they might also run a feature article. Yes! I'm ecstatic.

I called Miami to talk to my special friend Craig Robins to seek his counsel, and a woman answered the phone. When I told her my name was Jon Jacobs, she asked, "Is that the fairy tale character?" I said, "Yes, that's me!"

I feel like things are going to continue happening and explode into the big time. This is how I'm interpreting the Omens. However, even if things take longer, everything that has and is happening is laying a tremendously solid foundation for developing further relations with the media.

My fingers are crossed!

Boy oh boy, I am *nutz* with excitement and daydreaming. *Is it really going to actually happen, big time?* Am I finally, after eighteen years of being an actor, going to get noticed? Despite all my efforts and faith in my Destiny, the reality of the possibility takes my breath away. But, *it could happen*. I mean, this is what I've been working for. This is my dream.

How about this? My friend Craig just called me back from Miami and heard my news. As he was about to put the phone down, he said, "Christina really came through for you, didn't she?" At first, I didn't know what he was talking about, but it turns out that the girl who answered the phone, the one who asked me about my name being Jon Jacobs, her name is Christina. So there we have another Omen on top of the last one. Does this mean that Christina at *The LA Times* will also come through for me, as Christina Fulton did when she gave such a fabulous performance in *The Girl With the Hungry Eyes?*

I forgot to mention that when I walked in today, the first message on my machine began with Jana, the girl who has done all the artwork for the movies, singing "John Jacob Jingleheimer Schmidt." This is all pretty wild, verging on delusional, don't you think? But then again, this is the whole point of this book: to relate how Omens actually occur day-to-day and are the magical signposts in our lives.

1 February 1996

I went to Warner Brothers Music and had a good meeting with Richard Gitlin, Mimi Polk's husband. Perhaps he'll call me to do some kind of a music video, maybe using my short films for source material. Nothing obvious but a positive interaction.

I heard that the review from *The LA Reader* is mixed to good, pinpointing the technical aspects as weak and the performances as "erotically charged passion," or something to that effect. I'll have to wait a couple of weeks before it comes out. Besides that, I did a little voice-over for a vegetarian cooking show as a favour. It was a fairly amusing exercise. I don't think I experienced any profound Omens today.

3 February 1996

I was reading Carl Jung's *Memories, Dreams, Reflections* and something struck me. I had leapt ahead to the final chapter, where he espouses on the psyche of the individual who must strike out from the pack, and I grew excited—I felt as if I were reading about myself.

Then, to illustrate his point, he told the story of Jacob wrestling the angel. Another Omen. Does it suggest that *Welcome Says the Angel*, the movie in which I make my debut as an actor, shall serve to break me out onto the world stage? A wishful interpretation, perhaps, but it certainly suggests something profound. Just consider the poster. The fact that the public will see the name Jacobs associated with an angel could strike profound chords with the public. We will see.

On this subject, I'm reminded of an incident a few weeks ago when I was in a bagel shop talking to my friend Michael. I noticed a newsletter on the counter that discussed another myth regarding Jacob creating angels.

Between John Jacob Jingleheimer and Jacob's angels, I'm experiencing rather a bizarre synchronicity. I shall have to research both stories deeply. Meanwhile, is this an Omen of profound recognition coming my way in relation to this film, or is it simply a personal message to me to keep my faith and trust in my Destiny? Or is it both?

4 February 1996

Okay, this one is really bizarre. About ten days ago, I picked up a family to take to the airport. The woman's name was Christina and her husband's name is Joseph. We got talking and it turns out he is an Academy Award–winning composer of the song *You Light Up My Life*. He also wrote, directed, and produced the film of the same title, which grossed approximately thirty million dollars at the box office. He won the Oscar, the Emmy, the Golden Globe, and the Grammy for his song. He also co-financed and composed the soundtrack for *Lords of Flatbush*, starring Sylvester Stallone and Henry Winkler.

I picked Joseph up from the airport today and it seems that even without seeing the film, he really wants to compose some songs for *Welcome Says the Angel*, re-score it, and probably arrange the financing for the remix. He absolutely seems to want to do this. As it happens, we have a very weak score and would probably benefit greatly from this. I just need to show him the film and confirm with the director and producer that they are interested in doing this. It's really too early to comprehend what impact this will have on the film, but Joseph seems to think it could make the film a hit, on a major scale. He could be right. Let's see where this one's going.

And he very kindly gave me a twenty-dollar tip!

5 February 1996

I took a bit of a knock this morning. Christina at *The LA Times* didn't share Kevin Thomas's enthusiasm for *Welcome Says the Angel*, so it doesn't appear they will do an editorial story on the film. And now I find myself concerned that Kevin Thomas's review may only amount to a couple of lines, as opposed to a full two-column review. So I was bummed. However, as I was driving up to drop off a copy of the film at Joseph Brooks's place, in the middle of my malaise, I looked up and saw the name on the van driving ahead of me was Angel Appliances. So I shall fight to remain positive.

This morning my next door neighbour Chance told me he had met an old publicist who was interested in helping out. So I sent him a package. I also spoke to

Philippe, the director, last night, and he gave his blessing to the possibility of Joseph writing a theme song.

Time to chill out. I could hardly sleep last night, I was so hyped and obsessed. I think my daydreaming is running too far ahead and leading me to get disappointed.

I called the woman at *The LA Times*, Christina McKenna, and left her a message. She called back and said she liked the film, but she couldn't write about it because Kevin Thomas was doing it. So perhaps I shouldn't worry.

6 February 1996

I feel a little weird today. The publicist Chance introduced me to, felt like a real sleaze, which is unfair to say because I only spoke to him on the phone. However, suddenly I felt like I was promoting a sleazy film, instead of the beautiful film that it is. I read today that a movie called *Angels and Insects* opened very well in New York this weekend. Perhaps that is a good sign.

Joseph Brooks, the composer, watched the film. Although he is still inspired, he's not sure if this film isn't too explicit to get a wide release, so he's calmed down a little. This suits me, because I'd rather not make any decisions 'til after I read the reviews.

I took the famous Lloyd Bridges to the airport today. He was very sweet, as was his wife. He gave me a two-dollar tip; I shall keep one of the dollar bills as a memento. His son Jeff Bridges stars in the movie *White Squall,* which was produced by Mimi Polk.

Adam gave me his pages of the script we are writing together, so at least that is under way. I'm still fretting over the question of how extensive *The LA Times* review is going to be. I need to chill on that count.

I've been reading more of Carl Jung's work. How I love his muse. What a truly inspirational mind and being. His work makes me realize the potential value of this book, only in that few people, if any, have documented their path in relation to the details I'm looking for. I do hope my achievements on my path to fame are going to be of exception, so that people will actually be interested in my observations and how they might be applied to their own lives.

A little note on the subject of "Jon the Actor":

I wish to bring certain mythical characters to life and in order for them to be convincing and human, it will require fine acting. Since I was a child, I have always wanted to perform. I have enjoyed tremendously the transcendence experienced in playing a role or performing well. I greatly enjoy the challenge I face to be great in a role, because I have never felt as though it were a simple exercise for me. I also believe I do have a certain aesthetic appreciation; therefore, the standards I think I set for myself are quite high. My experience is still so limited that I have a long way to go before I will even have the imagination to conceive of brilliant creative choices.

It is my great dream and passion, beyond all else, to see myself playing these roles on screen. And because I value so highly the profundity of spending one's life pursuing one's dreams, I find myself respecting greatly my vision and the joy it brings me to fulfill myself. So basically acting in film is my first and great passion and filmmaking and everything that goes along with it, is the means by which I get the opportunity to act.

8 February 1996

The first review is due to come out in *The LA Reader* today.

For some reason, the review was delayed until next week. I'm not sure why at this point, but perhaps it will work in our favour.

9 February 1996

I'm told *The LA Times* review will be out on Monday.

10 February 1996

Today I dropped flyers for the movie around town. I was often struck by images of angels across the city. Perhaps this is less an Omen and more of a clear sign of how popular the concept of angels is, but does it bode well for our movie?

11 February 1996

I awoke early this morning to do some work driving, but the van wouldn't start, so I have the day off. I then had tea with my friend Valerie, and her conversation quickly drifted to the subject of my friend Samantha, whom I have known for seven years. Valerie doesn't know consciously that Samantha and I are having an affair, but it seems she was compelled to discuss Samantha's personal life, opening my eyes further to what I have got myself involved in. This is definitely a sign to be very clear and not indulgent with this gift from the Universe. I was thinking only yesterday how amazing it is that Samantha and I have finally become intimate. (She phoned mid-sentence.) This year has been tremendously rewarding in the way of recognition and Destiny.

I spent the rest of the day with Samantha. We made love and discussed all the things I felt that were intended by the Universe to be the focal point of our communication, namely her direction in life.

I have been reading more of C. G. Jung's *Reflections*. I love this man.

12 February 1996

Last night I dreamt there was a section missing in *The LA Times* review about *Welcome Says the Angel*.

This morning, I awoke, showered, and took a ritualistic walk to the Rose Café. I bought *The LA Times*, a coffee, and then sat down and rolled a cigarette. I pulled out the Calendar section of the *Times* and saw on the front page in the Highlights column, "*Welcome Says the Angel* Is a Surprisingly Tender Love Story," reviewed on page 4 by Kevin Thomas. I lit my cigarette and turned to page 4. There I read the headline, "Tender *Angel* Manages to Find Love in All the Wrong Places."

I won't transcribe the entire review, but first, he said that "the wonder of this $17,000 feature is that it compares more favorably with the much-praised *Leaving Las Vegas* than you would imagine." He then says, "It is amazing that Dib, in his feature directorial debut, and his actors make us care as much as we do. There's a vulnerability and honesty to Joshua and Ana, and they are *beautifully played by Jacobs and Hauer*. Dib's subtle and graceful direction makes this essentially two character drama feel like a filmed play." He adds, "*Welcome Says the Angel* is *a winner* about seeming losers."

I came home and cried and laughed for at least an hour. It was such a tremendous relief. I was crying with joy and laughing because we have achieved this recognition, purely off our own backs, no big companies, just friends and passion.

The first Omen of the day occurred when I went for breakfast with Michael. We showed the review to a friend behind the counter and some other guy who heard my name started singing "John Jacob Jingleheimer Schmidt." Confirmation that some people instantly make the association.

Later, I went to pick up the broken-down van I drive for the car company, and it was stored under the number 142, which has been my lucky number since my childhood. (It was the number of my cubbyhole at a boarding school I went to when I was six years old.)

Some guy picked up a flyer from a friend at a shop and then gave him three Cuban coins as a token of good luck. My friend later gave the coins to me.

Today is also my mother's birthday, which makes the review a truly wonderful birthday present for my mom.

Aside from this, I tend to hear songs about angels a lot when I listen to the radio.

What is next?

13 February 1996

This morning I got a call from Philippe, the director of *Welcome Says the Angel*, and he is flying in from Egypt for the premiere. This means the premiere represents a full circle completion, everyone together again. This, I think, is a very powerful Omen because with completion come new beginnings.

14 February 1996

Philippe arrived, and we spent many inspiring hours talking.

15 February 1996

The big day. I went with Philippe to the Rose Café and the first paper to arrive was *The Hollywood Reporter.* They called it "a love it or hate it picture" and described myself and Ayesha as dull and dreary. That grounded me somewhat. *LA Weekly* came in the afternoon and it was a good solid review. *The LA Reader* came in later and this, too, was a good review. Both reacted to the chemistry of the actors.

A remarkable Omen occurred with *LA Weekly.* Halfway through the review, the critic made a Freudian slip and called me Nick. He must have been thinking of Nick Cage because of the similarities to *Leaving Las Vegas.* Even more amazing when you consider this is his Oscar year. Nick is also the ex-boyfriend of my ex-girlfriend.

I arrived at the theatre for the premiere, hoping for a hundred people at best. Samantha was with me, soothing my mind. Suddenly, I was seeing more and more people arrive. My heart started to pound because the line was just getting bigger and bigger. Fortunately, earlier in the day, the theatre had decided to put us in the largest room, with 250 seats, even though I was leaning towards taking a smaller room of 160 so we could get closer to a capacity audience. Fortunately, fate intervened. We sold 270 tickets, grossing 1,700 dollars on the opening night. The atmosphere was tremendous, and afterwards, everyone seemed to have been captivated by the performances. I felt like I was experiencing an extended orgasm.

16 February 1996

I woke up this morning feeling calmer, as though I was now going to start dealing with reality. Suddenly, I heard Philippe and Seth shouting outside the window. They came up shouting that we had a fantastic review in *Variety*. We also were in the Best of the Weekend section of *The LA Times*. Later in the morning, we got the *LA View* review, which was a beautiful rave, and we found ourselves Pick of the Week.

Michael, the producer, told me that some of his friends commented the film has some of the best sex scenes in cinema. Another friend of his, a wonderful director named Stephen Tolkien, said that he sees me as a star. Most of the reviews refer to the chemistry of the actors in the film, all comparing it heavily with *Leaving Las Vegas*. It has been an amazing day. It has brought all of my friends together again. We feel like we have truly broken through, which is now undeniable.

Tonight I'm going to the Sunset 5 to see how many of the general public turn up at midnight.

17 February 1996

Last night, about twelve people attended the midnight performance, which was a little disappointing. However, this evening a girl called Fatos turned up, with whom Philippe and I had hung out at Toi four years ago and had told the story of *Angel*, before we had even written it. Anyway, she had come to the theatre not knowing the film was playing there. She didn't even know we had actually made the film. So we watched it together, then went to Toi, and Philippe told her the story of our next project. It gave me a very powerful sense of both completion and new beginnings, and meeting her felt like a good Omen for our next film.

Later in the night, approximately twenty-four people showed up for the film. Midnight is a tough time slot. But my friends Andrea and Cliff came with some of their friends, including the Native American actor Billy Wirth. Billy liked the movie a lot and responded to my performance. I feel like we will all be working together soon. Billy and I also drew the same fortune from fortune cookies. It said, "You will soon be honored by someone you respect." So we took it as a sign that we are acknowledging each other.

19 February 1996

Now it's back to reality—I need to make some money to pay my rent next month. I am concerned about financing the future of this campaign. I have a lot of work to do. I have undoubtedly established credibility for myself as an actor, so now I must capitalize on it.

Philippe and I spent the evening with Fatos, the girl we met at the movie. A very special girl.

20 February 1996

I booked the ads for next week and then slept most of the day. I am feeling run down.

There is an unhappiness between Michael, my producing partner, and myself. He feels that I'm so busy promoting myself, I'm not giving others their due. To set the record straight, I should give a little background into my relationship with Michael.

We met in London in 1985. My friend Craig Robins had suggested to Michael that we meet. We spent only one day hanging out, but immediately it was apparent to me Michael was gifted. He was an aspiring actor and as he relayed to me his adventures of sneaking in and out of the stage doors of theatres in London's West End, I realized he had an uncanny gift of getting into places I would be too intimidated to enter. Such a feat was not lost on me and I knew at that moment, Michael was to play an important role in my life. His plan was to move to Hollywood when he had finished traveling Europe and Africa, and I told him I would see him there.

We did indeed meet in Hollywood a year and a half later in January 1987, but I only lasted a couple of months on that trip. Then about six months later, after I made my second short film in London and I realized what hard work it was to produce, direct, and act, I asked Michael to fly over and produce my third short film. He did and thus was born a very creative working relationship. Michael later started working as production executive at a mini-major studio and over the next five years we tried in vain to get a feature film made.

It wasn't until 1992, however, when a project we had been developing at his studio fell apart, that we finally were frustrated enough to just go out and make a feature film with whatever funds we could get our hands on. That was when I co-wrote *Welcome Says the Angel* with Philippe Dib, who got seventeen thousand dollars from family friends in Egypt. Michael proved to be more than up to the challenge of producing a movie with such limited funds. In fact he thrived on it; he had already produced a couple of million-dollar features and I think the freedom he enjoyed while working on a no-budget picture proved more creative and satisfying. We all had a ball making that film and remarkably Michael managed to line up the money to produce *The Girl with the Hungry Eyes* at the same time. Less than a month later we were in Miami doing it again, but this time with two hundred thousand dollars.

As you can see it's pretty apparent that Michael has been integral in what I have been doing and what I have been able to accomplish. I think that the mere fact he fulfills the often less than glamorous role of producing the films means that I often forget to credit him, especially when I'm dealing with the press, who typically are more interested in writing about the actors and directors. The bottom line is the films we have made together are accomplishments we share; they are not just my accomplishments.

21 February 1996

Philippe left this morning to return to Egypt. He hopes to return in a couple of months so we can work on our next film.

After he left, I checked my mail and found a copy of *Cinefantastique*, with the review calling *The Girl with the Hungry Eyes* "The Best Horror Film of '95."

I think it is an Omen that it arrives this morning, encouraging me to move forward dramatically with *Lucinda's Spell*. I have now received tremendous recognition for both the feature films I made, as actor, writer, and director. It seems pretty extraordinary to me.

22 February 1996

I'm running around doing what I can do to keep the ball rolling. I wonder if we'll get a crowd at the theatre this weekend?

A photographer called Maggie got hold of me. She says she has some photos of Ayesha, the leading actress we may be able to use. What's interesting is that I need some pictures of me for publicity purposes. Maybe she is the one to do them.

I need to start making some money soon, but I'm feeling a little washed out after many sleepless nights.

A woman, Slim Brandy (the mother of J. C. Brandy, with whom I later starred in three movies), suggested to Michael that she would like to put the film on as a play on Broadway. Could be interesting. I talked to my mom. She enjoyed the premiere and reading all the reviews very much.

I'm not seeing angels everywhere I look or hearing people sing "John Jacob Jingleheimer Smith," so I think things are settling back down. Nevertheless, what was accomplished in the last week was astonishing—the kind of exposure and recognition that will have reverberations for years to come.

23 February 1996

I called a small distribution company in London that is owned by a friend of mine, and his partner told me they had just read a review on the film in *Variety*. I quickly sent them a tape to see if they will open it in London.

My ex says she's setting up a meeting for us with Jon Peters next week to discuss getting Columbia Pictures to do a theatrical release of my film *Hungry Eyes*.

I'm going to the theatre tonight to see if there is any action.

Only fifteen people showed up. The plan is to cut our losses (or, perhaps, keep our winnings) and move on to the next city. However, we will play Saturday night, our farewell performance.

24 February 1996

My ex told me that Jon Peters talked to Sony Pictures, who said they have no interest in doing anything with *Hungry Eyes*, but he seems to want to help. I'm sure he has his reasons, but then, who doesn't?

Well, about thirty people turned up, which is not enough to pay for the ad in *LA Weekly*.

Joe Ritter called me. He is a guy I met at Starbucks who came to see the movie. I read his script, *The Secret Life of Scarlett B*. It was a very exciting read. He thinks I'd be right for the male lead. I like Joe. I believe it may well be his Destiny to bust through. He wrote *Toxic Avenger*, but unfortunately, he received no part of the profits. He doesn't have the money for *Scarlett B.*; however, so we will scheme together and see what we can come up with.

Joe worked with David Tattersall, my great friend and also the director of photography who shot my short films. This is a good sign. (Joe later directed me in my script *Hero Lover Fool*.)

It's very cold in LA right now. Brrrrr!

26 February 1996

I drove around and spent a hundred dollars on new *Angel* packages. The box office report from the theatre said there were only eighteen people on Saturday night.

I read another of Joe's scripts, which didn't move me. I guess I'm feeling a little down. I'm not sure of how to move things to the next level—i.e., making a new movie.

27 February 1996

I got a copy of *Hungry Eyes* over to my ex, so she can pass it on to Jon Peters. Otherwise all was quiet.

28 February 1996

This morning I talked to Joe De'morais, a friend of mine in London who is going to push to see if he can release *Angel* in England. I had breakfast with Adam and Blair, another friend who directed a vampire movie and with whom I also have a series of mystical connections. Anyway, I was so excited I made them both laugh. Adam is going to show my stuff to a manager friend of his. Blair took a head shot of me for reference, perhaps to act in his movie.

As I was walking home from breakfast, I bumped into Joe Ritter on the Boardwalk. He ended up coming over to my place and we talked a lot more. He also revealed that he originally wrote the male lead role in *Scarlett B.* with Nick Cage in mind. This is a powerful sign.

I went to meet Lloyd Bridges at the airport, but fortunately for him a limousine had also been booked, so I left him at baggage claim. However, a fan of his photographed Lloyd and me together as he exited the plane. Interesting.

Quite a powerful day overall. Cristina confirmed that Jon Peters had an assistant collect *The Girl With the Hungry Eyes* tape. Also, my friend in London is now interested in *Hungry Eyes*, so I have to look into the issue of rights.

1 March 1996

This morning I was thinking about my ex, so I called her. She told me Jon Peters wants to see some more of the press on *Hungry Eyes*, so I put a little package together. She showed me some scenes from a new Zalman King episode, "Lola," she is in. She is extraordinary.

I dropped into the American Film Market and had a two-minute meeting with Eleanor Powell, with whom I have nurtured a business relationship for many years. I got the impression now might be the time for a deal. I'll see her next week.

I feel like something amazing should happen, a deal should come into place, that I am truly ready in the eyes of God to make another movie. I just have to wait and see if God feels the same way.

2 March 1996

LA Village View printed a photograph of Ayesha and me in this week's magazine.

Sixteen people showed up for the film last night and seventeen showed up tonight—certainly not enough to justify extending the LA run.

I spent the evening with my lovely friend Samantha.

3 March 1996

I picked two tarot cards, both indicating I must root myself firmly to the Earth to prepare myself for what lies ahead, and that I must beware expectations.

5 March 1996

Once again, Mel Brooks returned my call. I hope we'll get together in May.

6 March 1996

Yesterday, I dropped in a tape and copies of the *Angel* reviews with a management company called Addis-Wechsler. Maybe someone will see me fit for representation.

This morning I bumped into Bob and Greg Laemmle at the airport. The significance of this as an Omen I cannot fathom (except, perhaps, that they might mention *Angel* to exhibitors while in Vegas at Show West).

7 March 1996

As I was walking home yesterday, I had a thought about how I am waiting for a phone call that will profoundly affect my future. Tonight I received a message from a gentleman by the name of Mike Billington, who I met at the premiere of *Angel*. He suggested he may be able to help finance my next project. Of course, a lot of water may need to go under the bridge before that happens, but it is the first phone call I have received of this nature in a long time, and I feel ready. So we will see.

8 March 1996

Uneventful in the way of Omens, but I feel great and the weather is beautiful.

I pitched *Lucinda's Spell* to Eleanor Powell at August Entertainment, a large foreign sales company. It was a good meeting. It will be interesting to see what happens.

10 March 1996

I dreamt the other night that I was at a bank applying for a one-hundred-thousand-dollar line of credit, and I felt that because I have bad credit I wouldn't get it, but the teller told me that I was applying at the right time.

I met with Joe Ritter and Michael Kastenbaum today. It was a good vibe. Michael has decided to spend the last twenty-eight thousand dollars he has in the bank making four movies for seven thousand dollars apiece. His vision is to build a movie studio from scratch. I think if anyone can do it, he can. Let's see if Michael is willing to back a project.

11 March 1996

I spent most of my day driving for a living. I struck up a conversation with the last woman I picked up. Her husband is a first AD (assistant director). Anyway, it turns out that he, like Joe Ritter, also won a student Academy Award and also made a low-budget independent feature and was totally exploited by Troma. Poor guy was wiped out.

12 March 1996

I am seriously having to cope with being annoyed by my driving job. Besides that, I have a few scripts and tapes out in the world and I am curious to see the reactions over the next week.

I called Margaret, Nick Wechsler's assistant, and she said she saw *Angel* and really liked it, and she has passed the tape onto some other people in the company. They will let me know.

Bret, a friend of mine who acted in *The Girl With the Hungry Eyes*, told me his pal at *Esquire* magazine had read the *Angel* reviews and will write an article.

13 March 1996

Today I met Nancy Bishop at *Venice* magazine. She wants to take a look at *Welcome Says the Angel*. When I arrived home, I visited Valerie and told her about *Venice* magazine. I was toying with one of her CDs when I suddenly noticed it was called *Angels in Venice*. That most definitely appears to be an Omen that something will, in fact, occur with *Venice* magazine.

15 March 1996

Between driving jobs, I came up with a story that will truly lend itself to being shot for little to no money. In addition, I really like it, and it will work very well for Joe to direct. Michael also seems to be enthused and may finance it.

19 March 1996

I've fully developed this story, which I have tentatively called *La La Love*, as in La La Land.

Yesterday was exceptionally wonderful in that I spent the day with the lovely Fatos, with whom I have had a series of unusual encounters. Besides the beautiful time we had together, it has occurred to me she may be right to play the girl in this new story. She also told me yesterday about her friendship with the actor Peter Greene, who is another of these Hollywood characters I seem to have a mysterious connection with. I have construed this to be an Omen. This may mean one or all of at least four things, including that this new story will get made and Fatos will be in it, that Peter Greene may also be in it, or that Peter and I will work together at a later date, or that my story has true validity and I should put myself behind it wholeheartedly. We will see.

Besides that, all seems fairly quiet. No firm responses from money people with regard to *Lucinda's Spell*, but at least there is definitely some activity.

20 March 1996

I met with Michael and Joe Ritter to discuss this new film. Michael committed eight thousand dollars to the project, so it is a go. I will get to star in a second movie. Michael is pretty determined to play the bad guy and it remains to be seen who will play the girl. Fatos happened by the Rose Café while I was there with Joe, and he seems to agree she looks right for the part. An Omen indeed, especially since I wanted them to have the opportunity to see her before I ask her to audition. But we will still have to audition her for Michael and Joe's sake.

21 March 1996

I was told today that someone took the reviews of *Angel* and the head shot of Ayesha to the casting people at New Line, who are casting Mike Figgis's (*Leaving Las Vegas*) next film. And it turns out they were already looking for both Ayesha and me. They even had a head shot of a much older actor called John Jacobs. So they're going to receive my head shot and a copy of the movie on Monday.

Michael, Joe, Fatos, and I all met yesterday to get the vibe. The atmosphere was good, but I am having trouble with the idea of Michael playing opposite me in the film. Also, it appears the others are not particularly interested in working with Peter Greene if he is difficult, which he may well be. This causes some conflict within me—choosing between my friends' well-being, my instinct to follow Omens, and my desire to get the movie made.

On reflection of these issues, I called Peter Greene and left a message on his machine to call me.

Peter did, in fact, call back and left a message on my machine. On further reflection and discussions with Michael, I realized it is better to make the film with Michael playing opposite me, because that will serve as inspiration for Michael to produce. This whole issue caused me some inner turmoil to say the least.

In the last few days, I have seen a couple of signs, including a dead bird, while I was on my way to meet with Michael and Joe. These Omens have made me feel the vulnerability of this situation, so I am concerned about nurturing it correctly.

22 March 1996

I spent a wonderful night with Fatos and am convinced she is right for the part.

23 March 1996

Yesterday, we formally cast Fatos in the movie, so the team is now in place. In addition, we watched the

Oscars and Nicholas Cage won Best Actor for *Leaving Las Vegas*. Based upon all the curious ties, I interpret this as a positive indication of the future. Why should the pattern not continue to project us on a similar trajectory?

24 March 1996

Today Michael, Joe, and I went over the script and greased the communication channels between us. All is on course. I then spent the night with Fatos, which continues to be wonderful.

25 March 1996

I spent the day with Fatos. We visited one of her acting classes. The vibe between us is great, as is our understanding of what we are sharing.

The outside world appears to be in a certain calm, no dramatic news as yet. The Omens of late all seem to be tied in to making this movie, which, for the time being, I shall call *The Hero, the Lover and the Fool*.

Today a man attacked me suddenly on the street. But perhaps because I didn't react aggressively, he mellowed out and let me pass. This is a significant Omen in relation to the story issues in this new film.

29 March 1996

I have had a few days off work and started writing the screenplay for the new film, which I plan to finish before April 15. Today I spoke with this guy Michael Billington, who is going to try and organize a deal to supply us with equipment to make this film. He is also trying to push *Lucinda's Spell*.

Another friend of mine, Joe Chavez—the boyfriend of Jana, who has done all the artwork for the movies—wants to put together a prospectus perhaps to raise the money for *Lucinda's* Spell. He is a hot venture capitalist.

I talked to Margaret over at Addis-Weschler. She said she is definitely a fan and sent a messenger over to pick up another copy of *Angel* to pass to someone in their casting division. Meanwhile, back at the farm, I am driving for a living again.

In addition, it must be noted I'm really enjoying writing this screenplay, which is now titled *Hero, Lover, Fool*.

5 April 1996

I completed the *Hero, Lover, Fool* screenplay two days ago. It took a grand total of six days to write an eighty-five-page script, which is a record for me.

Yesterday, Michael and I met with Mike Billington, but I'm not sure if it will work out. It is too complicated to structure a deal because Michael is now dedicated to building his company—tentatively titled Ideal Pictures—into a full-fledged movie studio. He wants to control the copyrights of the movies to be able to achieve that. Michael and I also met with Zalman King, who expressed interest in what we are doing. However, I'm not sure he's the right guy for our projects.

I've been spending time with Fatos, which is very enjoyable.

My designer friend Jana's boyfriend Joe really seems to want to raise the money for *Lucinda's Spell*. He is prepared to invest in starting his own venture capital company. If we can work it out, I think I'll go for it.

Welcome Says the Angel was officially booked into the Grand Illusion Theatre in Seattle for April 26.

We are planning to shoot *Hero* in mid-May.

And finally, the telephone number at which Joe Ritter can be reached in New York is the same combination of numbers as Ayesha Hauer's in LA. (Ayesha was my costar in Angel.) This could mean that *Hero* will be another *Angel* to me. Or that Ayesha and Joe will work together.

Finally, I could really use a serious cash influx.

6 April 1996

Michael read the screenplay for *Hero* and likes it very much.

Yesterday I talked with Tyger, the wife of my great friend David Tattersall. David was the director of photography on my first four short films and is an extraordinary DP. It is likely he will shoot the upcoming *Star Wars* trilogy for George Lucas. I called to see if he might be available to shoot *Hero, Lover, Fool*. Tyger said he is planning to be in LA at that time to begin preproduction on *Con Air,* a film to star none other than Nick Cage. The pattern continues.

I am highly irritable right now and feel like quitting my driving job. I find myself very graceless when dealing with my employers. I'm also very broke right now.

9 April 1996

Yesterday I met with Joe Chavez and we determined to embark on raising the money for *Lucinda's Spell* via a new company he is starting especially for this project called Motion Picture Capital. He feels it is destined.

Why should I not go with it? Especially considering I do not have any feelings to the contrary.

I put together all the materials for Seattle, which will be taking place on the 26th.

Margaret from Addis-Weschler called and said the people in casting over there still feel I am a hard sell on the acting front, not because of my acting, which they like, but because I am not involved in anything commercial as yet.

16 April 1996

I spent the weekend with Joe and Jana working on the brochure for *Lucinda's Spell*. Not only was it an inspiring time, but something quite interesting occurred. Jana, while coming up with a design idea, drew a sketch in chalk on her patio. The sketch somewhat resembled a pot of gold. When her next-door neighbour came home, she told us she had sketched a rainbow in the same place a few weeks before. Now, it just happens that the Christmas of 1994, Michael Kastenbaum gave me a book on leprechauns, and on the cover was a pot of gold at the end of a rainbow. That same Christmas, I was very broke and I made all my friends little clay sculptures. However, the one I made for Michael fell apart, so I rolled the pieces into balls, painted them gold, and put them in a box of sand—basically giving him a pot of gold. Now, just to cap it all, in the book Michael gave me there were several stories, and most of them told how people could never actually get the gold from the leprechaun. However, in the one story in which someone actually *did* get the leprechaun's gold, the person's name was *Jon Michael*. Something is definitely happening!

Yesterday I dreamt of my mother, and then she called and woke me up and said she was going to invest five thousand dollars into *Hero, Lover, Fool*. Also, when I spoke to her a week ago, she told me a psychic had told her my third film (*Hero, Lover, Fool*) will be the one that gets everyone's attention.

Is there magic in the air or what?

19 April 1996

Yesterday I printed up a revised version of the script and then left it on top of the van at the airport. It fell off. I take that as a warning sign to nurture this thing very carefully. Nothing else to report as yet.

20 April 1996

It appears Joe Chavez is going to have to spend twenty thousand dollars on lawyers to get everything set up legally for financing *Lucinda's*. He is willing to do this, so we continue to move forward.

I heard today that *The Seattle Stranger*, which is equivalent to *LA Weekly*, was very critical of *Welcome Says the Angel*. That brings me back down to Earth. However, any criticism right now will focus me upon the areas I need to pay special attention to on this next film.

Cliff Morrison called tonight and asked me to shoot him singing with the Lizard Son Band. I had a good time—he's a really talented guy without question. I wonder how his life will unfold. I wonder what the relevance is of my connection with the Morrison legend?

22 April 1996

I wouldn't say that any profound new Omens have occurred; however, things do appear to be moving forward. Mike Billington is now talking about shooting *Hero, Lover, Fool* on 35mm, which would up the budget to approximately one hundred thousand dollars, which is an exciting possibility. I'm meeting with his partner and him in the morning. Also, Joe is paying twenty thousand dollars on Friday to the lawyers to do the memorandum for *Lucinda's Spell.*

This definitely constitutes serious action on the behalf of the Universe. My toes, ears, eyes, and fingers are all crossed.

26 April 1996

Today is quite an extraordinary day—check it out! Joe paid the lawyer twenty thousand dollars on account of their work on the memorandum for *Lucinda's Spell.*

Welcome Says the Angel opens in Seattle tonight. I just called *The Seattle Times* and they confirmed they reviewed it today. I don't know what kind of review they gave.

Philippe flies in tonight from Egypt to begin working with me on our next screenplay. A bunch of Philippe's closest friends are also arriving today from Paris.

30 April 1996

Joe Ritter and Michael are both back in town. Philippe, too, has returned from Egypt, so there is a profound energy around. Philippe was critical of the script, but came through with some constructive observations.

Fatos has been working on her character and has strong feelings about changes that need to be made. I'm just struggling to keep up with it all. I feel a little drained but positive. I'm using some of the five thousand dollars to pay the rent for June so I can concentrate my energy on the film. I hope the money for *Lucinda's* starts to roll in.

I'm feeling a little sensitive with regard to my intimate relations with women. Perhaps I'm on the verge of growth and greater understanding of myself. This is a very delicate time. Much ground can be gained if the right steps are taken.

The reviews for *Angel* came through from Seattle. They were fair, but especially positive about the performances. However, the film grossed less than a hundred dollars in two midnight screenings.

I've not heard from the driving company, so I'm not earning at the moment, but I have so much on my mind I shall just leave it be.

Mike Billington has so far been unable to get clearance on financing the film, so we'll just have to see what happens.

3 May 1996

Okay, where to begin? I saw my ex the other day so she could sign a letter of intent for *Lucinda's Spell*. She confessed her continuing affection and bought me a pair of shoes because the ones I was wearing were falling apart.

Samantha and I had a talk about the fact that we dropped so quickly our newfound intimacy. She has just started teaching yoga, which is something I have been encouraging her to do, so I figure the way can explore our communication further is for me to go to her classes.

Mel Brooks called me at a moment when I was feeling pretty low. He was very nice, but said he didn't want to get involved in any outside projects.

Mike Billington called and said the deal is on! Yesterday we all had a meeting and an interesting thing came up. It turns out his partner VJ is a famous tennis player who Michael Kastenbaum had admired since he was a kid and who he has met briefly on several occasions (lines in airports, etc.). So I think that bodes well for the synchronicity.

They are due to put twenty-five thousand dollars in escrow by May 9. My fingers are crossed.

Meanwhile, I'm rewriting the script and feeling very pressured.

The process towards the financing of *Lucinda's Spell* continues to make progress.

7 May 1996

We went location scouting over the weekend and I found a little baby squirrel. A friend suggested I call it Oscar, which I did. An hour later, Oscar, one of my childhood friends with whom I haven't spoken for a while, called to share his life.

Yesterday at three A.M. I received a call from Peter Greene, the actor. He said he really wanted to be in the movie *Hero, Lover, Fool*. He called me again in the morning and reiterated that he should be in it and I shouldn't cast my friends all over the place.

Anyway, he hit a nerve, and with the support of Joe, the director, I talked to Michael about it. Michael was going to play the role Peter wants to take. Michael was initially angry, and said he would no longer play the part or put any money in, even if Peter withdrew. It was painful for me, but as I had previously thought, this was meant to be, so how could I not approach Michael about it? So we all had a meeting last night and Peter made his peace with Michael and impressed Joe, and so he is in, even though he hasn't yet read the script. This is truly exciting for me, because I have long wanted to act with him, and it really brings a serious edge to the film. So there are still a few more hurdles to cross, but things are certainly growing in stature.

Joe Chavez, who is going to raise the money for *Lucinda's Spell,* is moving things forward rapidly. I anticipate him having his operation in action by the end of the month.

The number one film at the U.S. box office this weekend was a story about witches, called *The Craft.* A good Omen for *Lucinda's Spell,* being that there is a demand for witches!

8 May 1996

I spent the night working with Peter and Fatos. We did improvisations until eight in the morning. All along the way, however, the script was being ripped to shreds and I was growing more stressed. But it was very exciting, even though our work was far from ideal.

9 May 1996

Peter began the day by wanting to get rid of the director. That night we all got together and it turned into a hell of a fight. Peter was intimidating everyone. He really wanted me to lose Joe Ritter, which I had no interest in doing.

10 May 1996

Stalemate. Peter demanded that I choose between him and Joe. I chose Joe. Peter has vanished, so that is that. I hope. However, his uncle Vincent did call from New York .

Joe says he hurt his back during a scuffle with Peter, so the shoot has been delayed and we need a DP.

11 May 1996

I called my father in London. He sounded much better.

The dead animal Omens, I believe, were the sign from the Universe to suggest the way things were going. I feel like I have just lived out my entire *Hero, Lover, Fool* script in reality. Making the film should be much easier.

13 May 1996

We went location scouting in Death Valley and found pretty much everything for the shoot. I am feeling a little heavy in my heart and mind, not having the kind of lighthearted fun I would like. However, upon reflection, I am rarely light about such matters. Nevertheless, I do feel ready. Fatos is in good spirits, as are Joe and Michael. What more can I ask? Unfortunately, the forty-thousand-dollar budget is not in the bank. There have been some delays, so I'm not sure what the budget is going to be.

Dear Universe, please enable me to give a wonderful and inspired performance, because at present, I have no idea how it will emerge.

14 May 1996

Michael gave our investors an ultimatum for Thursday. It looks like we will have to make the film for seven thousand dollars, or some such figure. I don't care, so long as we get out there and shoot something. All this procrastination is eating me up.

I received documents through the mail to sign for my screenplay company, Magic Screenplay. *Lucinda's Spell* is my only hope to survive after *Hero, Lover, Fool,* especially if Michael and I finance it, because I shall have to give my notice and will become homeless in the middle of June.

Trying to interpret the Omens is currently beyond me. I shall simply record the events as they unfold and we shall see where we are.

16 May 1996

The financing for *Hero* has not arrived. As a result, we are making the film for seven thousand dollars—thirty-five hundred dollars from Michael and thirty-five hundred dollars from me. However, Mike Billington did call today to say they are working on an alternative source of financing. For some reason, I am still optimistic, but not particularly worried which way it goes—so long as it goes.

I'm confident in the story, but not confident in my ability to act. I feel very stuck and out of tune. I really hope the Universe will guide me.

22 May 1996

It is now Wednesday. We start shooting on Saturday. Still, we have no more than seven thousand. We did a read-through last night that went well. I'm actually feeling confident in my ability to bring my role to life.

There have been no major Omens of late, except that last night was Michael's birthday and the production gave him a present of Robert Rodriguez's book *Rebel Without a Crew*. The cover artwork had been changed to feature Michael, me, and *Hero, Lover, Fool*. Who knows, it could be prophetic.

I went with Joe Chavez to the bank on Monday and we opened accounts for four of the corporations that will be involved in the financing of *Lucinda's Spell*, including Golden Shadow Pictures, the production company of which I am the sole shareholder. Joe opened the account with a thousand dollars, so to some extent, it could be said we have raised the first thousand of the two-million-dollar production and distribution budget.

24 May 1996

An additional twenty thousand dollars was committed today by Mike Billington and VJ for *Hero, Lover, Fool*. The contracts were signed. They offered us forty thousand dollars, but we decided to take only twenty thousand. If they like the work, they will finance another film for forty thousand dollars.

25 May 1996

We drove to Baker and shot the first scenes. I was pretty unhappy with myself to begin with.

26 May 1996

We filmed a bunch of car chases. It was fun, but I was still unhappy with my work. We acquired, via Margerette the makeup artist, two 1950s convertibles for the film. An absolute godsend.

27 May 1996

More car stuff. I've started to lighten up on myself. Joe appears to be doing exciting and humorous work, leaning heavily towards the action. Michael is proving to be a revelation as an actor. Fatos is doing wonderfully.

28 May 1996

The costume, which came together for me at the last moment, is heavily Western-oriented.

2 June 1996

Arrived back in LA at two A.M. I'm due to start filming exteriors today. Then two more days of shooting and we'll be on to postproduction. I'm excited we may have a great film.

4 June 1996

We completed the film today. The last scene took its own course and was filled with irony. It paralleled reality with extraordinary precision. I can only hope that my performance is special, because I was not exactly thrilled with my experience of myself in action. However, that only fuels my fire further. I'm determined to be a great actor.

5 June 1996

This morning I met with Joe Chavez to continue working on the financial package for *Lucinda's Spell*. All is on target. He gave me a thousand dollars cash—five hundred for my rent and five hundred for the Golden Shadow account. This is exactly what happened the day after shooting *Angel* four years ago: Cassian gave me a thousand dollars for *The Girl With the Hungry Eyes*. This is an incredibly positive Omen.

8 June 1996

I'm feeling like shit, very negative about myself. I really don't feel like I was any good in my film, which is a real disappointment to me when you consider how much it means to me. I also find myself a little uninspired with regard to the next film, with regard to what kind of a character to play. I find that I am bored of myself and not inspired to create another identity. Yuck!

I still haven't seen any dailies. Perhaps that's why I'm miserable.

I got together with Adam Cooper today and we worked out a story for a Western, which we plan to do in August. An unusual premise, I don't know where it's going yet. We shall just have to see. All I know is that Adam and I have a mystical connection and I shall have to trust in that.

Meanwhile, I must figure out a way to pull myself out of my current rut of negativity. Perhaps I need to start with getting healthy and truly fit.

Adam just called and read me the first half page of our script. I like it. That cheered me up.

9 June 1996

I worked with Adam this morning. We reached page four. I then spent the afternoon with Samantha and company in Topanga Canyon. Then I had dinner with David Tattersall, my friend who is shooting *Con Air*, a seventy-million-dollar film starring Nicholas Cage. David is due to start filming the *Star Wars* trilogy in February, so I need to shoot *Lucinda's Spell* before then if I'm going to have the chance to work with him.

13 June 1996

I'm feeling much lighter about the work I did. I've seen some of it, though I have heard nothing, as the dialog has still to be synced up. I haven't worked with Adam for a few days. I must confess, the story that we have devised is not exactly strong enough to promote for the twenty-thousand-dollar budget.

I'm gonna write another scenario, which the Universe kindly visited upon me, called *The Wooden Gun*. This lends itself perfectly to the themes that are strongest within me.

All is quiet on the woman front.

Tomorrow I meet with our investors to discuss postproduction on *Hero, Lover, Fool* and to confirm financing for the next one.

Joe, my partner on *Lucinda's Spell*, is also moving things forward nicely, so we should see some serious financial action by mid-July.

Cash is currently low, so I'm considering driving again. Unless I decide to get a thousand-dollar advance for the next project, which might be worth considering.

I fell asleep this afternoon and dreamt of a monkey eating smoked salmon sandwiches. That is the closest thing to an Omen that has occurred of late. So onward ho!

16 June 1996

Yesterday was the wrap party for *Hero, Lover, Fool*. I finally saw the footage of the last major scene. It looked great, so now all that remains is to see how the thing works with sound. Yesterday Michael and I pitched our *Hero* investors with a silly mystery suspense story, which they had asked us for. They agreed to do it, so it looks like we'll be making another forty-thousand-dollar film in three to four weeks. We will see. The investors—Mike Billington, VJ Armitraj, and Max—also feel ninety-nine percent certain they want to finance *The Wooden Gun*. They appear to want to make approximately ten low-budget films with us and then move on to bigger budgets.

17 June 1996

I went to the gym and worked out, then went to a meeting with Michael and Max to go over the contracts. All seems well, even though Michael was being pretty tough in his demands. I got home to find a letter from my mom with another twelve-hundred-dollar investment in my next movie. We are also trying to get Max to buy us out of the last movie, in order to sweeten their contract. That would increase my working capital to thirty-five hundred dollars.

19 June 1996, Las Vegas, Nevada

I'm in Las Vegas with Michael. He is writing the script for the next movie, *En Garde!* I have been wandering around losing my money. It sure pisses me off. Down 250 dollars so far, 60 dollars left. Anyway, I'm probably miserable enough to start writing now.

So I shall work on *The Wooden Gun*. It seems if we can get these two scripts written we will actually get to make them both in the next twelve weeks.

22 June 1996, Cody, Wyoming

I'm currently on the seventy-thousand-acre ranch that belongs to one Bo Polk, who was, at one time, the president and CEO of MGM Studios. I'm checking it out as a potential location for *The Wooden Gun*. Cowboy art and memorabilia surround me. On the bathroom walls hangs a collection of letters to Bo from President George Bush. Bo is the father of Mimi and Steven.

23 June 1996, Cody, Wyoming

I rode for five hours yesterday and two hours today. My rump and the inside of my legs are sore, but I seem to be able to manage riding fairly well. Michael is finishing writing *En Garde!* However, I'm not sure that either of us will be inspired enough to want to make it. At this point, I'm more interested in focusing upon writing the Western *The Wooden Gun*. The story is classical in nature and only has to be creatively executed to be compelling. I must confess, I still feel a lethargy upon me, which I need to shake off if I'm to get some serious work done. I also hope that if we withdraw from making *En Garde!* that it will not seriously damage our relationship with VJ and Max of First Serve Entertainment.

28 June 1996, Venice Beach, California

I'm at home now. We backed out from making the *En Garde!* film, which I am pleased about. Max of First Serve didn't appear to be too disappointed with our decision not to make it. Only time will tell if more financing is forthcoming....

I am currently battling with my tendency to feel severely disappointed with my performance in *Hero, Lover, Fool*, which I honestly think is dreadful at this point. Whether good editing and looping can save me, I don't know.

I joined an expensive gym at a hotel to encourage myself to live a healthier life. I know I look much better on film if I'm fit.

The contracts for *Lucinda's Spell* are now all in place. I actually signed away the script yesterday. We shall see if the first money starts to roll in over the next four weeks.

My agenda is now to finish *The Wooden Gun* script in July and recover my confidence as an actor.

7 July 1996

I'm feeling like shit. I'm so disappointed with my performance in *Hero, Lover, Fool,* it has taken the wind out of my sails. I haven't been working out or writing, and I've been screwing around with a computer game, which totally sucks the life out of me and drains my energy.

I'm seriously questioning my creative relationship with Michael, because it doesn't appear that our acting together is very complimentary. So I have to rediscover my discipline. I'm inclined to finish writing the Western and perhaps have Michael direct it if he insists on being seriously involved. That way I write this whole period off as a learning experience and forget about results.

Overall, a fairly negative state of mind.

The only thing that is exciting right now is that Joe should have everything in hand by Monday the 15th to enable him to start raising money for *Lucinda's Spell*. He has spent approximately fifty thousand dollars so far.

8 July 1996

Okay, I'm feeling better today. We are going to start tightening the film up tonight. Max went directly to Joe Ritter this weekend and suggested reshooting. It's funny that he didn't call me to discuss his thoughts. Perhaps they will pull out. Who knows?

11 July 1996

We screened a revised cut of *Hero, Lover, Fool* last night and it went down very well. It looks like our investors will continue to finance the postproduction. The story comes through very clearly, so it is now time for me to stop worrying about it.

What I must do now is concentrate and get some work done.

14 July 1996

Yesterday we finished editing. Seeing my work pissed me off no end again, and I awoke filled with tremendous negativity.

So I went to see Eddie Murphy's film *The Nutty Professor* and that cheered me up. However, I definitely take no pleasure in being at home and feel the need for a big change of life.

Also there are no special romances going on for me and so I feel dull. I need to cure my acting flaws *tout de suite*. That will probably elevate my mood.

No new Omens to report. I just have to see what happens. Money next, and then I can go visit my poor old dad in London. Then come back and make *Lucinda's Spell*.

16 July 1996

I went to a meeting with Joe and a potential *Lucinda's Spell* investor.

We had another screening of the film. The reaction seemed fairly positive. I didn't stay 'til the end. Instead, I went to see my ex and assist her with her *Melrose Place* script. I find myself totally attracted to her.

17 July 1996

Slept a lot throughout the day. Not feeling great. I'm currently at the editing suite and I'm experiencing a severe low. My energy is nonexistent, my inspiration impaired. I find my performance in this film without merit and uninteresting even to myself. Extremely negative thoughts running around my head. What a drag I feel. I'm barely able to concentrate on writing or upon completing the current project. Not very good at all. As of tomorrow, I think I shall have to focus solely upon my health and fitness, lest my lethargy overwhelm me entirely.

22 July 1996

I made a concerted effort not to do any writing this weekend to recover my inspiration and motivation. I watched a lot of films, particularly Clint Eastwood Westerns, which I love.

We have locked the picture on *Hero, Lover, Fool,* and so now I just have to do some looping and I can forget about it. I'm feeling a little better, but only a little. I still feel unhappy with my life, my day-to-day existence.

24 July 1996

I've managed to get a few pages done in the last two days, so that is encouraging.
Besides that my energy is still low and I probably need to change my lifestyle dramatically. This is a *must.* The Omen business is slow. It would be nice to see some bizarre episodes of coincidence occur. Joe is working on raising money for *Lucinda's Spell.* (A little prayer: Dear Universe, please help me discover what I need to do to improve my acting. And please help me do it. Thanks.)

25 July 1996

I just received a call from Gergely Fonyo, a very genuine guy from Hungary who worked as the first camera assistant on *Welcome Says the Angel* and *The Girl With the Hungry Eyes.* I have always thought very well of him and seriously considered him shooting *The Girl With the Hungry Eyes,* even though I'd never seen his work as a director of photography. I also recall that he was particularly encouraging and inspired by my work as an actor, and that is something I will always appreciate. Anyway, Gergely just called and said he has just finished writing his first screenplay and would like me to read it. In addition, he has me in mind for the lead role. I shall cross my fingers and pray it is a good script because I would love to work with him.

26 July 1996

I spent the day working on the postproduction for *Hero, Lover, Fool*. I made some progress, so it should get easier.

I read Gergely's script. It is lovely and inspiring. It needs to go a little further here and there, but I would like to act in it, so I shall definitely share my enthusiasm.

I met with Joe Chavez for dinner. Things are progressing with the financing for *Lucinda's*. I hope the money rolls in soon.

I'm going to write a few pages of *The Wooden Gun*, then go to sleep.

29 July 1996

I met with Gergely today. He wants me to play the lead in his film, which I think will be called *The Forever Child*. I will work with him to get the script right and we will see.

I'm almost finished with the first draft of *The Wooden Gun*, except that it will only run about fifty pages. But a little extra work will take care of that.

I feel extremely lazy. I talked to my dad today, he sounds very low. That makes me sad.

4 August 1996

Today I met with a filmmaker Sartaj Khan, who called me for some feedback on a film he is releasing himself, called *All Is Fair in Love and War*. He is an interesting guy. I don't know if he's talented, but you never know.

The negative for *Hero, Lover, Fool* has gone missing, which is a major disaster if we don't find it.

VJ and Max have decided they don't want to do a Western, so that leaves only Michael and me to finance *The Wooden Gun*. We will see about that. Joe Chavez is busy working on the financing for *Lucinda's Spell*.

Personally, I'm still not entirely inspired, which is too bad, but hopefully, I'll get my energy up soon. I still find myself turned on and off like a light switch when I'm around my ex, which is trouble. I need to stay clear of her.

9 August 1996

The negative for *Hero* has been found!

The first ten-thousand-dollar check arrived for *Lucinda's Spell*. Our first investor is a doctor from New York.

I met with Gergely last night, and we made a major discovery for his script. The title will be *Johnny Famous*. Basically, I will be playing myself, as I was when I was ten years old. I have a great silly rock 'n' roll song that I wrote in February, called "Johnny Famous," and we'll use it in the film.

Michael has confirmed he wants to make *The Wooden Gun*. Randala, my great friend and roommate, will play a mute Indian squaw. Things are looking better and I'm feeling more energetic.

17 August 1996

I'm quite excited about the Western, although I still have to deal with my self-discipline. I have cast Dawn Kapatos, the girl I met three times in one day, as one of the leads in *The Wooden Gun*.

No beautiful women in my love life. I'm feeling a bit lethargic, but I'm going to improve things.

I'm going to start a new section of this book, noting the amount of money in the *Lucinda's Spell* bank account:

Currently: $2,500   Target: $2,000,000

29 September 1996

I have just flown back from Cody, Wyoming, where I have been for the last three weeks filming *The Wooden Gun*. It was a tremendous experience. We shot the picture in black and white 16mm. I co-directed and played the lead role, Jake Finney. I think it was a breakthrough performance for me, in that I shattered my super-sensitive characterizations and became a fiery, unpredictable, and dangerous figure with a true cynical edge.

We had a mountain of support in Wyoming from the locals, including the local gunslinging troupe, who embraced us entirely and whose respect I won as a character. We also filmed in the actual Hole in the Wall cabin, which was the hideout of Butch Cassidy and company. The entire crew was moved deeply by the experience. Despite freezing cold conditions and sleeping in tents, it was certainly the warmest experience any of us have shared making a movie.

We haven't seen the footage yet. It remains in my closet, undeveloped, until Michael returns by car. Anyway, a very exciting experience. I have high hopes.

Meanwhile, things are continuing to move forward with *Lucinda's Spell*:

Currently: $7,500   Target: $2,000,000

More is due in on Monday. Generally, things look good on all fronts. We do have some technical problems with *Hero, Lover, Fool,* which we shall hopefully remedy *tout de suite.*

P.S. I drank a lot of Jack Daniels in Wyoming.

1 October 1996

I met with Joe last night and he gave me a couple of checks for *Lucinda's Spell,* which means that I'm in fair shape personally. I'm now focusing on postproduction for the week before I start work on the next film, *Mick and the Claw.*

Lucinda's Spell funds:

Currently: $15,000   Target: $2,000,000

3 October 1996

Mick and the Claw has been set for Oct 19th. It's written and directed by Kevin Hynes and is about an ex-rock star and an ex-pop star who are thrown together by their manager to write a hit song. In the meantime, I will deal with post on the other two films. *The Wooden Gun* was sent to the lab yesterday. We should start to see footage Monday or Tuesday.

My energy is slowly dwindling since I returned from Wyoming. I sent my father a Walkman today. I hope music will stimulate him. He sounds very depressed.

My great childhood friend Oscar O'Lochlainn is due in town tomorrow. He's playing guitar for Zoe, an English girl singer who's also a friend. Oscar may provide insights into my next character.

I paid Michael a five-thousand-dollar advance yesterday against his producer fee for *Lucinda's Spell*. I think that pleased him. Joe says his brother Vincent wants to open an office near San Diego to raise money for *Lucinda's Spell*.

10 October 1996

Yesterday we transferred the footage from *The Wooden Gun* to video so we can edit the film on computer. It looks tremendous. I'm thrilled and very excited. I just have to hope the sound is great and that the performances match their visual impact.

Meanwhile, my great friend Oscar was in town touring with Zoe. We all spent a couple of long nights partying, which was great. I hope it will inspire me for my next role as the Claw.

12 October 1996

I was in San Diego briefly today and I bumped into Vincent, Joe Chavez's brother, while he was out jogging. He enthusiastically anticipated that *Lucinda's Spell* would not take long to finance. We shall see.

I'm feeling good. I spent the day with Gergely, going through the script for *Johnny Famous*. I hope to start editing *The Wooden Gun* on Monday. *Mick and the Claw* has been postponed until October 26. A busy week, month, and rest of the year ahead.

23 October 1996

For the last ten days we have been editing *The Wooden Gun*, working around-the-clock on a friend's Avid. We just managed to complete the first cut, which is two-hours long, in time to submit it to the Sundance Film Festival. We also submitted *Hero, Lover, Fool*. We will see.

We screened the first cut of *The Wooden Gun* last night. Everyone liked it a lot. People liked my performance. Me, too. I have regained my confidence.

I discovered we start shooting *Mick and the Claw* tomorrow, as opposed to Saturday, which means I have only a few hours to prepare. And on that note, I must get back to work.

Lucinda's Spell funds:
Currently: $17,500   Target: $2,000,000

9 November 1996

I've just returned from Idlewild, where we filmed *Mick and the Claw*, which I think will probably be re-titled *Armadillo Man*. We shot for approximately thirteen days, and I feel it was another breakthrough performance for me. I was wild and crazed, and judging by the reactions on the set, very funny. I've not seen the picture with sound yet, but what I have seen looks promising. I think I'm finally beginning to find my feet as an actor. I have certainly cut loose.

People continue to react very positively to *The Wooden Gun*, so I am filled with optimism. In addition, I am due to start filming *Johnny Famous* at the beginning of December, so I shall have another opportunity to explore myself and the craft. I had a lot of fun working with everyone on the film, in particular Michael, cinematographer Scott Fuller, and the leading actress, Arrowyn.

There has been some movement on *Lucinda's* and may be more in the coming week.

Lucinda's Spell funds:

Currently: $20,000   Target: $2,000,000

10 November 1996

Michael threw a fit over at the offices of First Serve Entertainment. They had taken possession of the negative of *Hero, Lover, Fool*. Things were resolved, however.

12 November 1996

I'm feeling somewhat run down lately and I have much to do to prepare for the next film, and also some thought to give to the final cut of *The Wooden Gun*.

On *Lucinda's Spell*, Joe told me yesterday we have a hundred-thousand-dollar check that is postdated the 18th, and another twenty thousand dollars from small investors. This is a step forward. I look forward to the checks clearing. I saw David Tattersall this weekend. He is the cinematographer with whom I made all my short films in London. He just completed *Con Air*, a seventy-million-dollar action film starring Nicholas Cage, John Malkovich, Ving Rhames, and Jon Cusack. It's produced by Simpson and Bruckheimer (*Top Gun, Red October*, etc.). David will be shooting the next *Star Wars* film, to be directed by George Lucas in April 1997. How inspiring: Here he is shooting seventy-million-dollar pictures while I make seven-thousand-dollar pictures. Hopefully, on *Lucinda's Spell*, our worlds will collide.

My ex says she will do a cameo in *Johnny Famous,* and I think Gergely is casting Dawn Kapatos opposite me as Amy Jo.

14 November 1996

I just watched *Billy Liar,* a fantastic film starring Tom Courtenay and directed by John Schlesinger. It is similar thematically to *Johnny Famous.* Watching the film made me realize both how much work I have to do to make this film special and how far I have already come in fulfilling my dreams.

I feel a tremendous desire to get this character of Johnny right. It is definitely the one to clearly enable me to get a full perspective of my range as an actor, even though I feel there is still much more for me to explore. But at least if I get this right, the way ahead will be open wide.

Lucinda's Spell funds:
Currently: $22,500   Target: $2,000,000

26 November 1996

Gergely decided to delay shooting *Johnny Famous* until after Christmas. I think he is having quite a job pulling everything together, however he appears to be extremely confident and excited.

I had an interesting meeting with writer Jonathan Gems, who wrote *Mars Attacks* and other interesting screenplays. He is about to direct his first film and we got together just to talk about how much can be done with very little money. Something may come of this, but I have no idea what.

The hundred-thousand-dollar check we got for *Lucinda's Spell* was incorrectly filled out, so we have been sent two alternative checks, one for twenty thousand and one for eighty thousand dollars. The twenty is due to clear tomorrow. I hope we will start to see the balance rise.

We are continuing to have problems with First Serve Entertainment. I don't know how this is going to resolve itself. I'm due to spend Thanksgiving with my ex at the Peninsula Hotel in Beverly Hills.

27 November 1996

Last night I attended a Zero Pictures (After much deliberation, Michael changed the name of his company from Ideal Pictures to Zero Pictures.) production meeting and talked a bit about distribution. People are definitely interested in giving us money, but if it will meet Michael's criteria is another question altogether. People stuck around for scenes from *The Wooden Gun* and they appeared to love it.

Two directors said they would like me to act in their films. I also saw Joe yesterday and got more checks for *Lucinda's Spell*. Also, Jonathan Gems left a message saying that he loved *The Girl With the Hungry Eyes*.

Lucinda's Spell funds:

Currently: $30,000   Target: $2,000,000

Myself and Christina Fulton on the set of The Girl with the Hungry Eyes.

Ayesha Hauer and I on the set of Welcome Says the Angel.

A lovely picture of Ayesha Hauer (daughter of Rutger Hauer) holding a necklace made by Uma that was used in the movie.

From left to right: Michael Kastenbaum, myself, and David Tattersall on the set of Moonlight Resurrection *(1987).*

Myself and directory of photography Scott Fuller on the set of
The Wooden Gun.

Dawn Kapatos, whom I met three times in one day. Later we starred together in The Wooden Gun *and* Johnny Famous.

Me as the Claw, an alcoholic rock-n-roll icon.

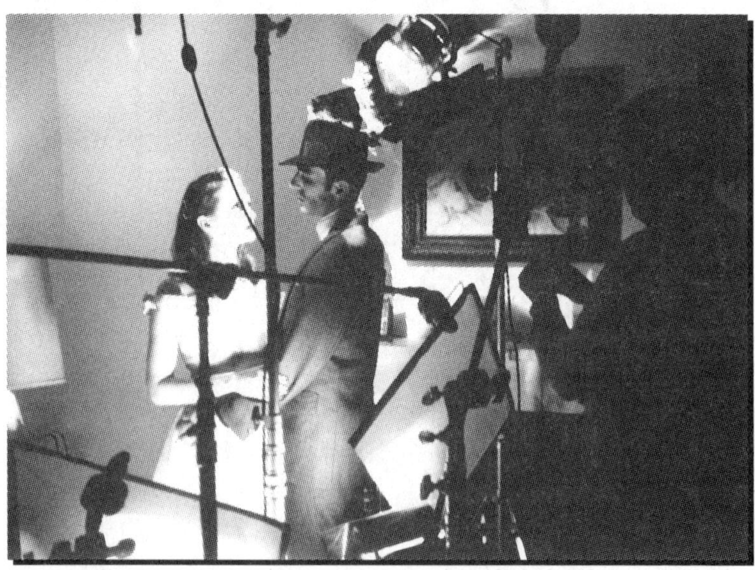

Dawn Kapatos and I on the set of Johnny Famous.

CHAPTER 3

COUNTDOWN

It's been a busy month. I went to London and finally saw my dad. He is pretty fragile. It was a lonely experience seeing him, but I know it did us both good.

London was expensive. None of my friends were around, so I ended up staying at a hotel in Green Park. I bought some props for *Johnny Famous* and a few ancient Egyptian beads to quell my peculiar hankering for antiquities.

I arrived back in LA and resumed editing *The Wooden Gun*. We almost finalized the cut but decided to sit on it for a month. Meanwhile, *Johnny Famous* is about to start filming next week, so now I'm starting to listen to 1950s music and get into character.

The big check for *Lucinda's* bounced, so that was a drag. However, it is the New Year and we are psyching ourselves up to make the film this fall with whatever cash is available, unless, of course, the Omens restrain me. Andy Peach, my storyboard artist friend, is flying out from London to work with me in February for at least three months. I'm very excited about that.

Lucinda's Spell funds:

Currently: $35,000   Target: $ 2,000,000

26 January 1997

I've almost finished shooting *Johnny Famous*. It's gone pretty well. I don't yet know how I come across, but Gergely seems happy. I am optimistic that the film may turn out exceptionally well, but we shall see. Last night I did a dream sequence with Dawn in which we were playing 1940s-style movie stars. She looked like Vivian Leigh. This felt like the payoff moment for all the magic I felt about Dawn. The Omens were correct: She was indeed to be a special person in my life. It was a magical moment.

Ayesha's manager, Carey Jones, called me and we are meeting on Tuesday. I feel ready to have someone representing me as an actor out in the Hollyjungle. Perhaps he's the man for the job.

A very interesting thing occurred, which is most definitely an Omen. I don't know where it will lead exactly. Back on 19 June 1995, I met a beautiful girl called Anna. I made a note of it in this book and have tried to make sense of it. Anyway, a few weeks ago, Randala gave me a head shot of a girl named Anna, who she met at the gym. Randala thought I would like Anna, so I called her the other day to set up a meeting to consider her for a small part in *Johnny Famous*. Only during our conversation did it occur to me that it may well be the same girl I met eighteen months ago. I won't know for sure 'til I see her in person, but this could be significant.

Joe says there are a few checks due to clear for *Lucinda's.* I hope so.

17 March 1997

My computer went down so I haven't bothered to keep things up to date, so I shall do my best to backtrack.

Anna Rakel *did* turn out to be the same girl whom I met so long ago. However, she didn't bother to meet up with me, so nothing has come of our collisions to date.

I finished filming *Johnny Famous.* It went well. In fact, I saw the first rough cut a couple of days ago and the film plays very simply. I was pleased with my performance. I actually found it somewhat sublime.

Andy arrived from London on February 4, and we have been working on the storyboards for *Lucinda's Spell* since then. They are turning out very beautifully. I'm thrilled.

The first cut of *Mick and the Claw* has also turned out brilliantly, so on the acting front it is going beautifully.

I went to Slim Brandy's Valentine's Day party and met her daughter JC Brandy and JC's fiancé Wick Coleman. We talked about filmmaking all night.

My father went into a coma on February 18 after suffering another massive stroke. He died as I was driving back from a meeting, at approximately the same moment I saw a truck with a big London emblem on it saying "Call now!" I went to London the next day, and to the funeral. I spent time with his brother's family, who I hardly know. His brother was very sweet, just like my dad. It moved me. I experienced plenty of emotion, but all positive stuff. I am happy he is free.

I collected about fifteen-hundred dollars from his bank account, as well as his papers and his unpublished short stories. I gathered the remnants of his art collection, then quickly got on the plane back to LA. Altogether, I was in London for eight days.

When I got back, my friend Sophie handed me a screenplay she had been writing with me in mind to play the lead. It is called *Dogstar,* about an autistic young man who is the embodiment of the brightest star, Sirius. His birthday is February 7, the same as my father's, and also the last day I spoke to my dad. We are going to shoot the film at the end of June.

I already invested the fifteen hundred dollars. It is a sure sign from my father, and will be my tribute to him. Tears pour as I type. We may look forward to the making of this film and all the magic it will continue to bring.

Since I got back from London I've been cycling to Starbucks in Pacific Palisades every morning to get fit. It's working.

Joe has been working hard on raising the money for *Lucinda's Spell*. I'm thinking we should start shooting in November.

Lucinda's Spell funds:
Currently: $85,000   Target: $2,000,000

20 March 1997

I've been offered the lead in a film called *Blue Door,* which shoots April 4. I will be acting opposite JC Brandy, the girl I met on Valentine's Day. She's producing the film. I'm gonna do it.

24 March 1997

For the last two nights, I dreamt about the new *Star Wars* trilogy, which my friend David Tattersall is shooting. The first night, I dreamt that I had directed one and was awaiting the opening night and feeling a tremendous pressure at the prospect of it failing. The second night, I dreamt David had shot all three films by June and was ready to shoot *Lucinda's Spell*. His hair was long and he looked like a teenager. We were both laughing and happy. David was taking the initiative and getting things ready for me.

I really love Venice; it's certainly my favourite place in the world right now. I find myself fantasizing of winning Academy Awards as I ride my bicycle. Aside from that, I'm feeling decidedly lazy. And there are no beautiful women around for me to romance. My ex is elusive. Tonight is the Academy Awards. I wonder if there will be any Omens for me.

25 March 1997

I watched the Academy Awards last night and did indeed find an interesting Omen. At the end of a sequence of old movies featuring Shakespearean quotes, John Wayne turned and said, "All's well that ends well." Now here's why it's interesting. Yesterday I was feeling a need to connect with my father, and so I looked through his papers and found a short story that looked interesting. It had something to do with inheritance, and so I went out for lunch and read it. Nothing particularly profound struck me about the story except that a man is surprised to find that he inherits a fortune from a rich uncle. It was a whimsical tale and I suppose I was attracted to it because my father left no will or any hand-written message for me and I guess one wants to find something somewhere. Also, yesterday I received a letter from the home in which he was staying. He had left a grand total of approximately fifty dollars in their safe-keeping, which they were asking me to donate. Of course, I shall. They also asked if there was a will, so I guess that was on my mind. Anyway, the short story about the inheritance was called "All's Well That Ends Well." So it is certainly bizarre that it should appear so profoundly during the Oscar ceremony. It is my wishful thinking that leads me to believe that my father has left me, in his esoteric and cryptic will, an Oscar waiting with my name on it.

Could it also be that since it was John Wayne who delivered the message, that it is a sign I shall win one for my performance in the Western *The Wooden Gun?* Boy oh boy, what an imagination this boy has. I rather like this interpretation because it's bold and exciting.

26 March 1997

Today I read in a magazine article that Ralph Fiennes' next movie is called *Oscar & Lucinda.* There's a nice little bit of insanity for my book. I feel like Nostradamus.

Aside from that, there is an attractive girl, Kelly, who lives next door, but no Omens to connect us.

I talked to my mom. She dreamed that my ex and I were getting married and were going to have a baby. My mom also said a psychic told her I could make a lot of money from the Internet. Not much else to report.

Except, perhaps, on my own state of mind, which I do feel the need to write about, probably for my own clarity. I'm going through a somewhat unfocused state currently. I cycle every morning and fantasize about getting famous, then I get home and usually feel unable to concentrate on anything. I feel great about *The Wooden Gun, Mick and the Claw,* and *Johnny Famous.* I'm sure they will garner me good reviews as an actor and cement for all time my accomplishment. However, I'm uncertain how much exposure I can generate for the films beyond opening them at the Sunset 5. I don't know if a distributor of any merit will take them on; nor do I know if we will have any success with the festivals. Also, there is still much postproduction work to be done on them and I'm not inclined to focus on that. I also find that with each new acting role, I am totally uncertain what shape my performance will take until I get to the bottom of the character, which I tend to delay 'til the last moment. Perhaps I should change that. My greatest concern with my acting is my ability to generate the furious inner energy that I so like to feel bubbling beneath the surface of an actor. Also, I must work on strengthening my voice, keep working on my fitness, learn to focus myself, and make a concerted effort to get my actor's kit (head shots and reel) done so that I know that I have left no stone unturned.

I've been spending too much money of late, money I've earned for my screenplay *Lucinda's Spell.* Thus far, I've received twenty-seven thousand dollars and it's gone! Seventy-two fifty went into films, but the rest has just gone into living and indulging. I must train myself to save.

There are no new love interests, and my social life is as retarded as ever. Randala is still sharing the apartment and, even though her company is constantly rewarding, I certainly desire to live alone.

I would like the money for *Lucinda's Spell* to roll in faster so I can make firm commitments to some of the talent I would like to attach to the film. Even as I write this, however, I can see there are benefits to preparing for a low budget. In fact, even the full 1.5 million is very little in conventional cinematic terms, so the more practical the approach I take, the better prepared we shall be.

Things are really very good. I truly feel I have achieved a certain greatness in my acting, which I now must strive to develop, deepen, and expand. People are offering me roles, which will continue as I continue to do good work. I still feel good about my father's journey beyond the material plain, however. I shall probably be reflecting upon that for the rest of my life.

Ron DeBlasio, a record producer and manager friend of Randala's, just called and invited her and me to dinner tomorrow. Could be interesting.

1 April 1997

I went with Randala to Ron DeBlasio's place. I showed him and a band called the Young Dubliners some scenes from *Mick and the Claw.* They all seemed to get into it. In fact, the band members were blown away that it was me playing the Claw—they didn't even recognize me.

Last night Michael screened *Mick and the Claw,* and the reaction was similar. People appear to be blown away by my performance. I feel certain that I will get the kind of acting reviews that I need to establish me as a serious contender. This is truly a major turnaround in my life. It is even a massive step forward from the reaction to my performance in *Welcome Says the Angel.* It will be very interesting to see if things work out the way I see it. I'm certainly daydreaming fiercely, projecting positive images for myself.

I got into a bit of a debate with my ex with regard to our relationship. I told her I didn't want to see her anymore on a personal basis because she's flaked on me so many times.

2 April 1997

I cycled up to Temescal Canyon and put some more dough in the bank for *Lucinda's Spell*. There should be some more cash this week.

Lucinda's Spell funds:

Currently: $87,500   Target: $2,000,000

I'm in a furiously bad mood. I find myself irritated by the fact that I'm sharing my apartment with Randala. Nothing personal, but I just want to do my own thing in my own space. I'm still having trouble focusing on my character preparation for *Blue Door*.

The weight of distribution sits on my shoulders like a ocean liner's anchor. Barring acceptance at film festivals, which has eluded me since my earliest short films, the only hope of exposure seems to be self-distribution, a task of epic proportions with respect to making a profit and actually cracking the hype market. I'm feeling such frustration. I'm sure Randala's feeling it, too, but she must act accordingly. I shall have to endeavor not to push her away with my foul moods.

AGGGGGGGGGHHHH!

3 April 1997

I'm getting ready to leave for Carmel to shoot *The Blue Door*. I'm still feeling weird and moody and low. I have no idea what kind of character will emerge in the next day, nor do I have any idea what kind of a performance I will give. I find myself longing for love.

12 April 1997

I got back from Carmel a couple of days ago. I don't feel like I was able to do much with the role, but I did have fun. Who knows, perhaps there will be a few good moments. It was certainly a very dirty movie, lots of sex.

As soon as I got back, I was struck by my usual lethargy and a fierce anger at the fact that I have to share my apartment with Randala. My ex called me from Paris, despite the fact I've asked her to leave me alone. She was doing her normal sweet and tender routine that she fails to back up with commitment. There are currently three women in my house and they are aggravating the shit out of me. I don't want anyone in my house.

I joined Gold's Gym to start a new era in fitness. The only Omen of late I can think of is that Kelly, the attractive girl who lives in the building next door, slept in my bed while I was away filming. Perhaps that is "a preview to a coming attraction," as my business partner Joe Chavez would say.

15 April 1997

I've been shooting extra scenes for *Johnny Famous* for the last few days. I feel like Charlie Chaplin as I do my funny walk along Venice Beach boardwalk.

I've been hankering after Kelly, the girl who lives next door. I hung around over the weekend and told her I like her, but she has a boyfriend and is totally pre-occupied at the moment, so I'm endeavoring to just let it be. Perhaps her situation will change.

Besides that, I'm generally distracted, as usual. I've been working out at the gym. I still feel somewhat over-whelmed by all the distribution work ahead. I'm running low on cash. I hope Joe will bring some more in soon. The storyboards for *Lucinda's* are going beauti-fully. No new Omens that I can recall.

18 April 1997

Sophie cast JC as the female lead in *Dogstar*. Tonight I'm introducing them to my next-door neighbour Gabriel Jewel, to consider him for the role of Astro, my brother.

I'm feeling a little better, perhaps because I'm actually not doing anything. Also, I had another look at the first cut of *Johnny Famous* and I'm very pleased with my per-formance. I'm pretty much settled on the idea of shooting *Lucinda's Spell* in November with whatever is in the bank. Currently, the actual account balance is 47,700 dollars. I've spent money on storyboards and other preproduction expenses. Scarily enough, we have actually now hit the ninety-thousand-dollar marker in terms of what has actually gone into the account. I've gone through approximately seventy thousand dollars since August, which is horrifying. A quick breakdown of those expenses goes as follows:

storyboards through August	$14,000
Michael advance	$5,000
film investments	$7,250
lawyer	$2,000
Randala script editing	$2,000

gym	$1,000
trips to England	$5,000
production design	$900
taxes	$3,500
car	$1,500
cameras	$1,000
computers	$1,500
rent	$6,500
phone	$3,000
miscellaneous purchases	$3,000
other production stuff	$2,000
artwork and design	$4,000

This leaves about seven thousand dollars for expenses. More money than I've ever had in my life, passing like water through my fingers. Thank God I've actually been productive.

Lucinda's Spell funds:

Currently: $90,000   Target: $2,000,000

21 April 1997

I went to *The Blue Door* wrap party on Saturday, then some of us went on to Las Vegas and had a wild time, to say the least. An interesting Omen struck me. The opening chapter of this book is called Zero Hero, and Zero is the name of Michael's company, through which he has been producing all these films. So to have viewed myself as a Zero Hero was somewhat of an Omen. Anyway, let's see what happens this week.

23 April 1997

A profound Omen has been evolving over the last few weeks, which is difficult to interpret simplistically.

It revolves around the number sixty-nine, which is featured heavily in the *Lucinda's Spell* story. Jana, me, and Andy were trying to come up with a magical symbol to use to market the film, in the same way the bat insignia is used in the marketing of Batman. We have also been trying to figure out what tattoo Lucinda should have on her butt, and I had this flash it should be the number sixty-nine, which is possibly a little crass, but it is also means fun to me. Anyway, it turns out the number sixty-nine on its side is pretty much the astrological symbol for Cancer, which is my ex's star sign. Also, my moon is in Cancer, and the two most important relationships of my life have been with Cancer women, so I take this as a clear sign to use the number sixty-nine prominently in the marketing campaign. I also feel this is a profound sign from the Universe that everything I'm thinking in this film is more deeply rooted than I might imagine. I really do equate the making of this film with some of the major turning points in cinema.

Today I saw a dead cat on the side of the street, which I took as a sign to be careful in my play. Also, I realized my character in *Lucinda's Spell* is not that much different from Travis Buckle in *Taxi Driver*.

24 April 1997

A good Omen occurred yesterday. After reading Spielberg's biography, I was thinking how exciting it is that David is to be the director of photography for *Star Wars*. And then today, as I was browsing in a movie memorabilia store, I found a press kit for the film *Moll Flanders,* which David shot. I leafed through to see his bio. To my pleasure, I discovered *Metropolis Apocalypse,* a short that I directed and which played at the Cannes

Film Festival in 1988, was included amongst his list of accomplishments.

Michael was given a flyer for a preview of a movie playing tonight, which is plotted very similarly to *Lucinda's Spell*. I hope I have not been plagiarized, although, if I have, I shall take it as a compliment.

28 April 1997

The movie was sold out, so we didn't get to see if it was similar to *Lucinda's*. I shall not worry about that.

Lately I find I'm very excited about making *Lucinda's Spell* and challenged to make it visually a truly exciting work.

No Omens that I can think of have occurred in the last few days, but all is well, if a little slow. I have been watching Spielberg films lately.

30 April 1997

A series of Omens occurred that are definitely interesting. Yesterday I was having coffee at the Coffee Bean Café, and I bumped into Scott Fuller's ex-girlfriend Deborah, who is also Mickey Rourke's ex-wife. We chatted, and then I cycled over to the gym. As I was cycling, I was daydreaming about running into Mickey and asking him if he read *Lucinda's Spell*, which I had given him to read two and a half years ago in Miami. So I pull up outside the gym and there's Mickey. But I didn't feel like talking to him because I knew he wouldn't recognize me and I wasn't in the mood to be awkwardly trying to remind him of our last conversation. Anyway, we worked out right next to each other in the gym, and I felt like it was a good sign that our paths should be crossing again.

When I got home, I mentioned this to my partner Joe Chavez, and I said I really only wanted to approach actors if our paths smack us right into each other. Joe then mentioned he had seen Peter Greene in a film a few days ago and liked his work a lot. I explained that Peter was a handful, but that if our paths crossed, I would certainly be open. I found myself daydreaming that if I bumped into him, I would shake him hard and tell him to pull his shit together so we could get some work done.

Last night I went to a screening of a short film at the AFI and Peter Greene is standing in the parking lot. This was the first time I had seen him since the *Hero, Lover, Fool* fiasco. So I went up to him and gave him a big hug. He apologized and said he really would like to work with me. I felt a genuine respect and warmth from him. The Universe, it seems, does have it planned for us to work together, because I felt no fear. I am aware of the risks, however, the possibility is definitely still alive. And then this morning I went to the gym and found myself working out next to Jean-Claude Van Damme, whom I have also met before. I didn't say anything to him, but I feel like the Universe is speaking to me.

Yesterday I saw *The Blue Door* dailies. It looks good, but I think my performance lacks imagination, confidence, and nuance. It's not terrible, just below par. Time to reflect.

3 May 1997

Yesterday a bird shit on my head. That, I believe, is a good sign. Also, a spider crawled up my arm, which is supposed to be a good sign for money. Besides that, I saw *The Big Blue* yesterday, which I found inspiring in relation to *Dogstar*.

I continue to have a definite crush on Kelly, the girl next door, but she's still in a relationship.

4 May 1997

Kelly invited me over for tea. She soon let it be known that she had broken up with her boyfriend, so it appears the way is open. Now, just to be sure she likes me.

7 May 1997

The latest in the Kelly saga is that I dropped by her place the other night and she was with a new lover, so that cooled me off a bit. Unless she is clearly flirtatious, I shall discontinue my overt courtship and simply see if she will come to me.

On the *Lucinda's* front, I called Tyger Tattersall. She is definitely supportive of *Lucinda's Spell,* but there will be no firm commitment from David until after he has finished shooting *Star Wars.*

I met a guy the other night at Michael's place who is a director. He loved my performance in *Mick and the Claw.* He really thinks I should get an agent. Also, I saw the new cut of *Johnny Famous* the other day. Gergely has added much of my humorous scenes and it plays beautifully. I'm very excited by the whole thing.

12 May 1997

Today there was a headline in *Daily Variety,* under the Cannes Film Festival section, that said "Dogstar Catches Fox." It was in reference to a film company called Dogstar, but I felt it was a good sign. Perhaps *Dogstar* will be at Cannes next year.

William Patnosh, the young director who liked my performance in *Mick and the Claw,* saw my performance in *Johnny Famous* last night and has since asked me to read for his film, *Poets Mission.* I'll see him Wednesday.

I met with Michael Kastenbaum today to discuss the Zero Pictures deal for *Lucinda's Spell.* I think we will be able to work something out. I'm meeting with Joe Chavez tonight. I understand we have a few more bucks in the bank.

15 May 1997

I just experienced a wicked Omen as I was driving along Wilshire Boulevard. I had stopped at a red light when I noticed a large bird flying above the road with a smaller bird chasing it and hassling it. I knew immediately that it meant something, because it was such an unusual sight. I was trying to determine if the smaller bird was a magpie, which is not a good sign because the song for magpies starts, "One for sorrow, two for joy." Anyway, as I was staring at the birds—*smash!* I got badly rear ended. Ultimately, four cars were involved. It appears that some poor guy had a seizure and lost control a couple of cars back. Anyway, I was caught in a sandwich. But what a spot-on Omen. Actually, only a few days ago I witnessed a similar accident and wondered for a brief moment if it was an Omen, but I brushed it off.

Lucinda's Spell funds:
Currently: $95,000   Target: $2,000,000

16 May 1997

It has occurred to me to note that because the cost of financing *Lucinda's Spell* is so high, we have, in fact, raised four hundred thousand dollars so far for the film. However, the majority of the first four hundred thousand dollars has gone to start-up costs and sales commissions. The film, however, will now start to enjoy fifty percent of all monies raised, so, with the blessing of the Gods, our budget should start to rise more rapidly.

18 May 1997

Randala returned to Europe today, leaving me my apartment to myself. I feel great and inclined to rediscover my discipline and sense of myself.

The other day I broke my resolve not to approach Kelly, and I attempted to corner her with regard to her feelings. She said she is emotionally distracted, and I've heard rumors that she is pissed off with me for cornering her in her apartment.

My mom mentioned the other day she dreamt I played Mel Gibson's brother in a movie.

Lucinda's Spell funds:

Currently: $ 97,500   Target: $2,000,000

25 May 1997

Today I got my eyes tested and got contact lenses and designer glasses. I have long avoided taking care of this and perhaps good things will come as a result. The woman selling me the glasses gave me a discount, and the figure she quoted was 669 dollars, which is also the first three digits of Lucinda's telephone number. So despite the fact it was much more money than I had intended to spend, I felt it was a good Omen and I went for it.

26 May 1997

I partied again last night. I don't think I ever partied so much in my life. It is a funny double-edged sword in the respect that it allows you to enjoy a wonderful closeness with people, but it takes its toll on your energy and clarity. Life is funny like that, so full of paradoxes.

I find it difficult to break out of my habitual routines. I go to such extremes. I'm obsessed with my work; however, I'm lazy to the point of inertia. Despite all this, I don't feel so bad at all at this moment. In fact, I feel rather inspired. I would like a girlfriend, but I love living alone. Yes, I'm basically still a young man and have more to do before I will be ready to maintain a domestic situation.

Some pigeons found their way into Andy's apartment and shit on the storyboards. This is a good Omen!

28 May 1997

The magic continues to feel very strong in my life. My biggest challenge is myself. I'm due to resume editing *The Wooden Gun* this week. Besides that, not much is new, except that another check came in today.

Lucinda's Spell funds:

Currently: $100,000   Target: $2,000,000

4 June 1997

I'm not sure if there are any profound Omens to report. I did find myself renting a documentary on the life of Bruce Lee, and I started thinking perhaps it might be my Destiny to die young. Quite a few crows and ravens have crossed my path lately, but this thought was fleeting and I feel there is still much I'm meant to do before my time's up.

I find myself almost exhausted by my daydreams lately. I'm constantly thinking about being famous and willing myself to be a great actor. I hope this is positive thinking and not just procrastination. I mostly have these thoughts when I'm working out or walking or driving, so I guess I'm in action.

Things look promising on the financial front for *Lucinda's*. Some deals are in the works. The storyboards are also going very well.

Lucinda's Spell funds:

Currently: $105,000   Target: $2,000,000

6 June 1997

I saw *Con Air* today, and I feel a tremendous excitement about working with David Tattersall. Great things for the future feel inevitable. Also, a lot of my lucky numbers came up today in receipts and the date 06/06/97.

The only sad thing is that I have no lover with whom to celebrate. Oh, well. Soon!

9 June 1997

Con Air opened in the number one spot this weekend, grossing 25.5 million dollars and pushing Steven Spielberg's *Lost World* to number two. David called me, and I was delighted to be the one to tell him the film was number one. We talked a little about *Lucinda's Spell*.

I'm very optimistic he will make the time to do it, and it will be the first of many feature films we will make together.

I almost got hit by a car today. I have definitely been experiencing Omens to remind me of my mortality.

15 June 1997

Sophie Pegrum who is directing the movie *Dogstar* had a couple of dreams about me—one with Paul McCartney and then another with Nick Cage. I'm not sure what the significance is.

Through a little magic, I met a film editor I think might be great for *Lucinda's Spell* but I'm too lazy to go into detail. His name is Clayton Halsey; we will see if he figures down the line.

16 June 1997

I edited my acting reel today and I'm very excited about it. It shows range—big time!

I saw Joe. Things look good. Also, I deposited a check today.

Lucinda's Spell funds:
Currently: $120,000   Target: $2,000,000

25 June 1997

Not much has occurred in the last week, except that I feel I need to make my actors reel tighter. Also, we finished cutting *The Wooden Gun,* so now the emphasis will be on sound and music.

I dreamt last night that I was robbed while I was sleeping in my car and that my ex was somehow involved.

An investor is flying in tomorrow to meet with Joe. He has already invested a hundred thousand dollars. Joe is hoping to get as much as an extra four hundred thousand dollars. I will also be meeting him. This will be interesting.

It's now time for me to focus on *Dogstar*. I would like to be able to elevate my work to a finer level. That would certainly be encouraging.

2 July 1997

I caught a leaf falling from a tree and made a wish for *Dogstar* to be a great film and for me to give a great performance. I rarely manage to catch leaves; that in itself is a good Omen. Meanwhile, I'm still preparing the *Dogstar* character.

Joe's meeting with the four-hundred-thousand-dollar investor went very well. He has agreed to put up a half million dollars. Joe will be working on getting that into the bank while I'm away. My fingers are crossed. That would bolster the budget very nicely.

My mother called and gave me the number of a girl who works at DreamWorks, Spielberg's company. My mum met her mum in the Bahamas. My mother had also had a dream about me doing something with DreamWorks, so I just put in a call because I'm too superstitious not to, even though I find it a little embarrassing.

I've been offered another leading role in a thriller called *Prometheus Bound*, which will start shooting in August. I would play the role of a psychotic killer. I'm not sure if I will do it yet, but for experience's sake and to explore my dark side, I shall consider it. In addition, it was written by JC Brandy and her fiancé Wick. Meanwhile more money has filtered in for *Lucinda's Spell*.

Lucinda's Spell funds:

Currently: $135,000   Target: $2,000,000

22 July 1997

I have just returned from Colorado, where we shot *Dogstar*. It was quite an emotional and tough shoot for some. For myself, it was tough only in that I had to maintain a pretty intense emotional and creative state for most of the picture. I would say at this point that it was my most creative performance. I was concerned my character was a little too understated as written, and I was not confident in my ability to carry a picture in that fashion. I found myself exploring a multitude of characterizations, so hopefully, the emotional center will keep the character grounded. If so, it could turn out to be my best film.

Meanwhile, I've accepted *Prometheus Bound*, which starts in three weeks. Also, my mom and sister are in town. Joe's been working hard lately, and we have more in the bank.

Lucinda's Spell funds:

Currently: $175,000   Target: $2,000,000

28 July 1997

I am starting to become Jason, my character in *Lucinda's Spell*. It was not intentional, and therefore worthy of consideration as an Omen I will be able to bring depth to my performance.

A really brilliant guy, Gabriel Jewel, lives in the next apartment building. His magnetic and gregarious personality has always struck me as inspired. During one of our long conversations, he was telling me about some events in his life that I interpreted as positive Omens. Anyway, Gabs has not been pursuing any creative artistic outlets, and instead he has been building a small business and enjoying himself. On a number of occasions, I found myself encouraging him to think about his passions. Then, when Sophie wrote the script for *Dogstar*, it struck me Gabs might be perfect to play the role of Astro, my brother. Sophie agreed and Gabs was cast. He turned out to be a natural and was an absolute pleasure to work with. He and I especially had a good time.

Since then, I still find myself inspired by him and look forward to working with him again. When we were at the beach yesterday for the *Dogstar* wrap party, Gabs and Sophie suddenly discovered they have many mutual friends in England. Also, Gabs mentioned for the first time that one of his first or second cousins is Vivien Leigh (*Gone with the Wind*). I think these little details, combined with the fact that it is great to find a good actor to work with, may portend to more films with Gabs in the future.

3 August 1997

Kelly flirted with me a little the other night, so there's still a chance of our being together at some point. However, she's still with her boyfriend.

I've hired a trainer to prepare me for *Lucinda's Spell*. I hope to get into my best shape ever. Joe's been working on a big deal for a few weeks; I hope he can pull it off, because we are getting very close now to preproduction. I intend to start casting at the beginning of September, as soon as I've finished *Prometheus Bound*.

I saw the dailies for *Dogstar*, and I was not over the moon. However, that does not mean it isn't going to be fantastic. Anyway, I was walking down the road in a bad mood and a fly buzzed into my ear. For the hell of it, I've decided to interpret it as a positive Omen that this film will cause quite a buzz!

2 September 1997

I just finished shooting *Prometheus Bound*. Although it didn't feel like my best work, it was certainly experimental and should provide me with insights as to what I can get away with.

Meanwhile, I have now started pre-preproduction on *Lucinda's Spell*. I have a hundred thousand dollars and am looking for people who can work with us at that level. I've seen a lot of sixty-nines on the Omen front, which I find encouraging. Full steam ahead!

Randala returns from England tomorrow.

3 September 1997

Tonight I had a strange compulsion to shave my chest in preparation for *Lucinda's Spell*. What a weird feeling it is to be like a teenager again. It's a good thing I did it now, because I'm pale and need a tan.

8 September 1997

I've been mailing out scripts and posting casting notices. Indeed, it is exciting to be pulling this production together. Sixty-nines are prominent. As I was glancing at one of the papers I was putting a casting notice in, I saw the name Necessity listed amongst the cast of a musical. Necessity is Lucinda's nickname. Also, I saw one of my scenes in *Dogstar* synced up. It played very well.

11 September 1997

I've been talking to some special effects companies and it appears we'll get a few nice effects relatively in-expensively.

It was my birthday yesterday and my friends arranged a surprise party for me. Ayesha Hauer called me yesterday to chat. I had her name on my list for people to consider for roles in *Lucinda's*, so I thought it a good Omen for her to call. So I cast her—as what, I haven't decided.

Joe is fired up. I'm optimistic the budget for *Lucinda's* will grow before we shoot. The team is looking good. It will be nice to get some fresh faces involved, too. Fhiona-Louise, my ex-ex from London, called today. I would like to cast her in a small role.

18 September 1997

Another five thousand dollars in the bank, which is always good news! And a couple of amusing Omens.

The other day, I mentioned to Andy and Jana, who are the production designers on the film, how when I was making my short films, I went as far as to have jewelry especially made for the films. Then today, Uma called me from Singapore to say hi. She was the one who made the jewelry—very magical pieces they were—and now she is going to make a piece for *Lucinda's*.

I was reading *The LA Times* and I found an article about a British actor, Steven Mackintosh, with whom I used to go to school. I cast him as my brother in my first feature *Pagan*, which ultimately never got made. I was pleased to be reading about him. It mentioned his wife's name is Lisa Jacobs, so I thought that was a good Omen.

I saw the final cut of *Johnny Famous* with music. It was really lovely and has real possibilities, as far as the festivals go. My fingers are crossed. Who knows, maybe even Sundance! (*Johnny Famous* indeed became a festival favourite, it also won Best Picture at the Hungarian Film Week, their equivalent of the Academy Awards, sharing a prize of 187,000 dollars. Gergely is Hungarian.)

We have set our start date for shooting *Lucinda's Spell*: November 22, 1997!

Lucinda's Spell funds:

Currently: $195,000   Target: $2,000,000

21 September 1997

I called David Tattersall this morning and spoke to Tyger. From our conversation, I gauged that David was very much in the process of figuring out his plans for the rest of the year. I called back a little later and made him an offer to shoot *Lucinda's Spell*, which he greeted with tremendous enthusiasm. I am so excited, I am over the moon! I believe together we can craft an extraordinary picture. Tyger will also be working on the film.
I then called Joe and he is going to cut me a check tomorrow to back my offer. The Universe is smiling on us, big time.

22 September 1997

Today I Fed Ex'd David's deal memo and a fat check for a three-week shoot. Joe immediately reimbursed me. Tyger called to say I must also petition for David's visa, so I called my lawyer and quickly agreed to the twenty-five-hundred-dollar fee. The reason I'm moving forward so quickly is to enable him to have the utmost confidence in me.

Three times people have said to me in the last few days, "It's all good," which I understand is an expression used frequently in New Orleans. I consider that a good Omen. I'm very aware of my thoughts of late and am quickly vanquishing any negative projections or fears from my mind.

28 September 1997

A very intense week. David's schedule is looking pretty hectic and as a result, I spent the week in a fever of thought. Today he called me to say he couldn't do *Lucinda's Spell*. I'd had a million conversations with him in my head, and even dreamed last night that he would call to say he couldn't do it, so I spewed out all the best thoughts that had come to me. At the end of our conversation, he was once again alive to the possibility of shooting the film, *Star Wars'* pickups permitting. Right now I'm calling Tyger to get his passport number, so I can get his work visa approved. All in all, I'm enjoying the challenge of getting him to New Orleans.

Today I heard fifteen minutes of the music for *The Wooden Gun* composed by Niki Jack. It sounds great, and of that I am truly pleased. I'll be spending the next two days meeting actors for *Lucinda's Spell*. On the

Omens front, all is quiet except for the proliferation of the number sixty-nine.

1 October 1997

I spent the last couple of days casting for *Lucinda's Spell*.

A very funny Omen occurred when I first arrived at Joe's offices in Century City. I noticed his parking space was right next to Michael Plotkin's space. Michael was the attorney on *The Girl With the Hungry Eyes*. The relevance of this is that I have come full circle, in that this time *I* control the future of the film and there is no one involved who doesn't truly believe in the project. Aside from that, I met some good people. Also, we got some more dough in the bank and more in the pipeline.

David, as I understand, is still on the ropes. He did pass on his passport number, however, so I should be able to get the visa in place. Today I sent him some of my movies and the storyboards, so perhaps that will encourage him.

Lucinda's Spell funds:

Currently: $205,000   Target: $2,000,000

5 October 1997

The other day, I was walking down Third Street in Santa Monica, thinking about what an incredible game life is, and a guy walked past me wearing a Sundance Film Festival T-shirt. It felt like an Omen that at least one of my films will be accepted this year. Some more money also came in this week, which is good news.

David called me today to once again to express his reservations about doing *Lucinda's Spell*. It appears the

Star Wars pickups may be shot in December. So we had a lovely talk, as usual, but this time I decided to back off. I simply said I will assume he is not going to be able to do it, but he may call me to say he can do it if he wishes. In some respects, I feel like I should keep fighting, but I don't want to ruin our friendship; instead, I will just let go. If it's meant to be, it will happen.

Lucinda's Spell funds:

Currently: $215,000   Target: $2,000,000

6 October 1997

It was a little sad to tell Joe that David is going to rip up the fat check I wrote to him to shoot *Lucinda's Spell*. Personally, I'm not worried about doing the film without him, but I wish there were something I could do or say that would inspire him to just do it! Nevertheless, I shall move on.

14 October 1997

I just got back from New York, where I did a cameo in my friend Bret Carr's film. I didn't feel any connection with the material, and I had a hard time memorizing lines, but I got through it. I arrived back to find that my car had been stolen, which is unquestionably an Omen of change.

The vibe is good with regard to New Orleans. It appears there will be plenty of support from the local community. We already have some people lined up. There is also more dough in the pipeline, upon which I'll report further when it hits my account. The sixty-nine Omens continue to appear.

On Saturday, I'm due to see David Tattersall, after which I'll know for sure if he's going to shoot the film or if someone else is going to. Also, I'm feeling the need to have another breakthrough on the acting front to make this an entirely memorable performance.

24 October 1997, New Orleans, Louisiana

I'm in New Orleans. We are in official preproduction on *Lucinda's Spell*. So far, it is just me, Michael, Andy, Jana, and Truman, who is Michael's assistant. David Tattersall and I met on Monday night, and it was clear he was not going to do the film. Scott Fuller, the DP who shot *The Wooden Gun*, also decided he couldn't do it.

So the job has gone to Jaime Reynoso, who shot *The Blue Door*, *Dogstar*, and *Prometheus Bound*. He is a tremendously positive guy, and very sweet and talented…a little inexperienced, but it feels like the right move. Sixty-nine has figured prominently, as usual.

Joe put the money he had fronted for David into the movie, so our production budget jumped to 154,000 dollars. Things are good. I just need to go to the gym every day.

Lucinda's Spell funds:

Currently: $220,000   Target: $2,000,000

25 October 1997

I've been in New Orleans for four days and I've gotten smashed every night. I have definitely become Jason, the First Horn. In fact, when I wrote *Lucinda's Spell*, I really was writing what I believed to be a fictional character for myself to play, but here I am now living my character.

There are so many positive Omens I'm not sure I'll be able to list or remember them all during this intense production period. However, I'll note what I can. There are two streets in the French Quarter that correspond with names of characters in the film, Maddison and Ursula. The woman who lives in the house we may rent for the production may be perfect for a role in the film. The number of the building is 1469. Also, she mentioned her friendship with Chris Blackwell, who was my friend Craig's business partner for a while.

JC Brandy, my co-star in Blue Door, Dogstar, *and* Prometheus Bound.

My next-door-neighbor-turned-actor, Gabriel Jewel and I on the set of Dogstar. (Turns out he is related to Vivian Leigh.)

Kelly Williams (left) moves in next door and I am besotted. This ultimately leads to us co-starring in Randala's movie, Phoenix Point.

From L to R: Joe Chavez, Jana Pesek, Peter Pesek, Jon Jacobs, and Andy Peach. The last coffee at the Rose Cafe in Venice before we leave for New Orleans to make Lucinda's Spell.

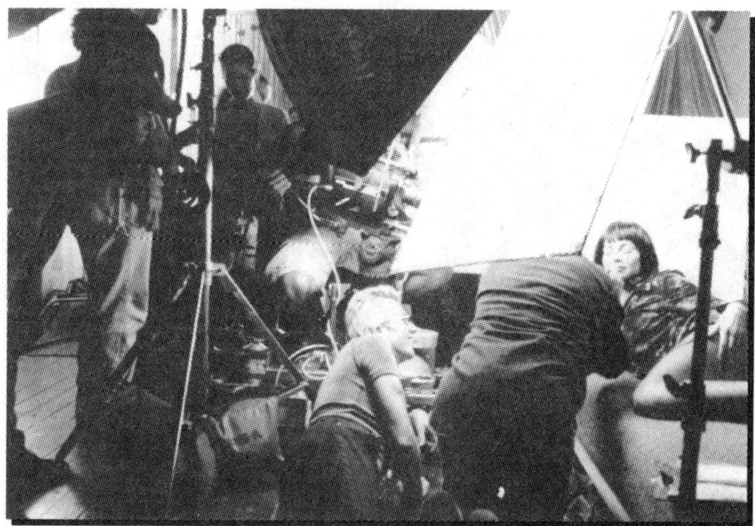

I'm lying on the floor directing a scene from Lucinda's Spell. Christina Fulton is on the couch getting a touch of makeup.

Tyger Tattersall and I in a New Orleans cemetery on the set of Lucinda's Spell. "Yes, it is real Jack Daniels!"

"Joe (the Champion) Chavez" and Jana Pesek get cuddly behind the scenes in New Orleans.

Michael Kastenbaum makes producing look easy.

CHAPTER 4

IN THE CAN(NES)

The computers all went down in New Orleans, so I was not able to update this book. Perhaps that is well, because it was too intense a period to be able to do anything other than wake up and shoot the movie. I shall endeavor to recall the pertinent details and bring things up to date over the next few entries.

Clayton Halsey, who is editing *Lucinda's Spell*, is cutting the final sequence together. Our first cut of the film is complete.

Today is the anniversary of my father's death, so I'm going out to dinner with my friend Randala to celebrate his memory.

15 March 1998

I have officially locked the picture on *Lucinda's Spell*, which means no more editing. I did what I could to tighten it up, but could not bear to cut too much out, so the running time is 106 minutes. I had a few test screenings, and the reaction was wonderful. People laughed throughout the movie. I have submitted it to the Cannes Film Festival, both to the main competition and the Semaine de la Critique.

This year marks the tenth anniversary since my first short film got into Cannes. I would like to think that is a good Omen. There have been other minor things to encourage me to believe the Universe is behind the film getting into Cannes. One thing is certain, it is a tremendous film, extremely fresh and entertaining, with unlimited potential. In addition, we have put together fabulous artwork and design to promote the film, which will really catch people's attention.

We have another six weeks of postproduction to get through. It is my mission to stand by this film to ensure it gets the widest possible release. A whole new realm lies beyond, a whole new way of life. *Cannes, here we come!*

21 March 1998

Of late, the most important thing that comes to mind is to play a serious game of hardball and fight to get *Lucinda's Spell* the widest possible release. This means ignoring all the nay-sayers who would like me to believe it has only limited theatrical potential. It also means resisting the temptation to sell the film before it has achieved any recognition, and before I can witness, first-hand, its effect on a full theatre of objective moviegoers. This means committing myself to waiting for a festival to respond, certainly to give it time. Then, after some serious marketing pumping, and hyping the film, and generating as much awareness as possible, entering into negotiations with distributors. Basically, if I don't believe this film is going to be a hit, why should anyone else?

24 March 1998

There have been a number of sixty-nine Omens of late, especially in relation to money. I received checks totaling sixty-nine thousand dollars for my company to finish postproduction and more is on the way.

On Monday, the day of the Academy Awards, I found myself cycling alongside Arnold Schwarzenegger and family on the bike path. I then saw him later in the evening on TV at the Academy Awards. I construe that as an Omen I will be there soon!

1 April 1998

I find that despite my desire for *Lucinda's Spell* to get into the Cannes Film Festival, I feel powerless to make it happen, in the same way that I was powerless to get David Tattersall to shoot *Lucinda's Spell*. However, David did at least visit the set, and his wife Tyger was a tremendous asset to the production, so certainly much was gained by my efforts and wishing. But with regard to Cannes, it simply lies in the hands of the gods.

Actually, something of an Omen did occur with regard to Cannes. I received a fax from a French subtitling company . They were soliciting work, and they must have gotten my number from the Cannes Film Festival, but I think they sent out faxes to everyone who submitted films. However, I shall act upon it and start work on my continuity script so as to have a head start on the translation, if indeed we do get into Cannes.

9 April 1998

Every morning since I received the fax from the subtitling company, I've been anticipating an early morning call or fax from the competition. This morning, one came in from the Directors' Fortnight. My heart was in my mouth as the paper sprouted from my fax machine. It was a gentle rejection, indicating they had already received too many American entries. I faxed them back to let them know that the director is British, not American, but I doubt that will make any difference.

Besides that, all is well. I currently have enough money in the bank to complete the film to show print stage. Creatively, the only unknown factor is the music and sound. I hope the team comes through.

One more note, I do now have a dialog script so that I can expedite the translation, if we do indeed get an invite.

11 April 1998

I just received the Omen that is the clearest indication that *Lucinda's Spell* is indeed going to Cannes this year. Earlier today, I was fantasizing about winning the Palm D'Or and Martin Scorcese, who is the head of the jury this year, handed it to me. Lovely fantasy. So then, just now, I was reading *Premiere* magazine, and there was an article about the "100 Most Powerful People in Hollywood." And who should be number sixty-nine, but Martin Scorcese? In the little blurb on him it mentions he is the head of the Cannes jury. As far as the Omens go, I would have to say that it all points towards Cannes.

14 April 1998

In view of the fact that there remains only one week before Cannes lists the official lineup, and all of the filmmakers involved probably already know about their participation, it is remarkable I am still so hopeful. I think it is my desire to manifest my invitation that leads me to such flights of fancy. I am inclined to record these little details so as to bring my thoughts into being.

15 April 1998

I called the main competition at Cannes today and they told me that *Lucinda's Spell* had not been accepted, and Directors' Fortnight have already declined. I called Critics' Week, and they said they couldn't tell me until Monday.

So the Palm D'Or is out, and now I'm wondering if I am indeed doing the right thing by not lining up a sales agent for Cannes. I shall reserve judgment until after Monday.

20 April 1998

I called the Critics' Week people today, and *Lucinda's* was not accepted, so Cannes didn't happen. So much for all my Omens. I guess they didn't mean Cannes. They can mean only one other thing: that all will go beautifully well and according to a scheme grander than my own.

I don't really care, when it comes right down to it. I don't feel the film was rejected; I just feel it didn't get past all the bullshit. So now my focus goes to finishing the film and submitting it to Toronto, Venice, Montreal, Locarno, etc.

23 April 1998

The score for the movie is finished, as is much of the sound work. Mainly, it is song licensing and looping still to go.

I am feeling slightly stressed out for some reason, but besides that, I feel great. Much better than two years ago. A lot more energy, for sure. I sort of realized today that things have certainly evolved for me. Whereas before we shot all the Zero movies, I was not sure of my acting ability; now I know I'm capable of all kinds of things and have most definitely demonstrated star quality in my movies. All that remains on that front is to actually get the films released and myself exposed. It will be interesting to see what comes up when I write my next screenplay. I feel like I shall be able to write even better scripts.

28 April 1998

Feeling a little low. Still licensing songs, etc. Experiencing a little doubt. Just have to remind myself to keep the faith. There's nothing to lose and everything to gain.

3 May 1998

My ex showed Brian DePalma a copy of the almost-finished *Lucinda's Spell* on videotape. I hear the evening went well, but she has yet to elaborate on his reaction.

7 May 1998

Two incredible Omens occurred yesterday and today. I got a call inviting *Lucinda's Spell* to play at the Cannes Film Festival in a nonofficial sidebar called

Cannes You Dig It? Film Festival sponsored by Slamdance. It is only the first year of this sidebar, and *Lucinda's Spell* is not yet ready to screen properly; however, we are going to do what is called a sneak preview and we will screen it on video. In addition, Jason McHugh, the organizer, loves the film and is really excited about it being there, and will give them film some kind of award.

What I love is that the Universe deviously came through and got me an invitation to Cannes. I think there's much potential here to build up the buzz for the film. Also, I think this will be great fun. I believe many things will come of this, not necessarily at Cannes, more likely after.

Also I had read about this festival in Variety a couple of weeks ago. So I know it has the potential to generate press.

There are many details with regard to Jason that I consider good Omens. His name is Jason, the same as the lead character in *Lucinda's*. He's of Scottish descent and his roommate's first name is Glasgow, and my character sounds like he's from Glasgow. Also, Jason produced a film and is good friends with Trey Parker and the other guys behind the hit TV show *South Park*. I have thought *South Park* would be the perfect place to advertise *Lucinda's Spell,* because it is the same target audience. The Cannes You Dig It? website will be connected to *South Park* in some way, and I'll have *Lucinda's* blurb on there. I love it! Yeah!

Now, check this out! We had sought a license to use the Jimi Hendrix song "Voodoo Chile" in the movie, but we had been warned the Hendrix family doesn't give festival licenses to Jimi's songs. Guess what! They faxed us, saying that because of a feeling of synchronicity on the part of Jimi's sister in connection with the storyline of the film and the story behind the song "Voodoo Chile," they decided to grant us the license. Yeah! Also, Jimi's sister is going to talk to me herself and tell me the story. Also, it is true that in 1966, when I was less than a year old, Jimi Hendrix and I lived in the same building and he used to make a fuss of me whenever he saw me.

31 May 1998

Okay, brace yourself. We went to Cannes and we *won* the Golden Warrior, the top prize at the Cannes You Dig It? Film Festival! From the moment I was invited, I collaborated with Jason McHugh, the festival's organizer. I paid for Guy Boss and Ade Pressly, a couple of DJs, to drive out from London to DJ our party, which I also co-financed. Even Christina Fulton flew in for one day. I took Samantha, Jana, and Kelly (the girl from next door) with me. The three girls dressed outrageously every day, and we got a lot of press and television coverage—Canal+, MTV Europe, Italian TV, French TV, Screen International, and Moving Pictures. The biggie, E! Entertainment Television, followed us for a whole day and recorded the awards ceremony. It is due to air on June 7 on their highest rated show of the year, *Sex on the Riviera.*

Since I got back, Joe placed a full-page ad in *Variety* congratulating the winners. I've had dialog with Leonard Klady at *Variety*, the guy who reviewed *Welcome Says the Angel,* and I think he's gonna be reviewing it this week. I also met one of the programmers for the Toronto Film Festival in Cannes, so we are well placed to get into Toronto.

Another interesting move I'm gonna make is to put some money into financing the theatrical release of Trey Parker's *Cannibal! The Musical*, which Jason McHugh produced. My main reason for this is to follow the *South Park* clues I've been receiving

Before I went to Cannes, I walked into a gallery and bought a bunch of paintings by a very cool artist named Dave Burke. I then met with him and showed him *Lucinda's Spell*, which he loved. He agreed to paint a picture for the poster. Somehow I think this also is going to lead to good things.

To summarize the past month, I would have to say we now have the publicity machine in first gear and a lot of new, interesting things are developing. We are moving in the right direction to make *Lucinda's Spell* a hit!

9 June 1998

Things move real quick. In terms of hype, we landed a full five minutes on E! TV's *Sex on the Riviera*. They showed clips from the film and we looked great and we were real. I had a meeting with my friend Greg Gardner, and that quickly led to a friend of his calling Josh Welsh, which could well lead to a big LA screening sponsored by the IFP (Independent Feature Project) West in their New Vision series. Also we have now locked the mixing facility for *Lucinda's Spell*, and that, too, seems aligned by fate. I received a fax from the Venice Film Fest asking me to correctly fill out their submission form. I consider it an Omen. I'm going to Venice, Italy, one way or the other. Leonard Klady is reviewing the film for *Variety*. He reviewed *Welcome Says the Angel*. Also, today Joe mentioned he has been running into the brother of David Hunter of *The Hollywood Reporter*, who reviewed both *Hungry Eyes* and *Angel* and who I particularly want to review *Lucinda's Spell*. I'm sure somewhere down the line something will come of that.

22 June 1998

I'm currently in the studio doing the final mix for *Lucinda's Spell*. It looks amazing on the big screen, really filling me with confidence that it will break out. I got another fax from the Venice Film Fest, giving me screening dates for submission, so I'm gonna fly the print into Rome personally. I've also submitted to Toronto this week, another major festival. In addition, I've had dialog with Rebecca Yeldham, a girl I know who is one of the Sundance programmers. Josh Welsh from the IFP West will see the print next week for consideration for their New Visions series. Joe's been raising plenty of cash for marketing, fueled by all the hype generated in Cannes.

The first review came out today in *Variety* by Leonard Klady. It was very positive, but not a rave. He didn't see the finished print with an audience, and I also figure he had too much personal contact with me to feel free to write objectively. Nevertheless, I pulled some good quotes out of it: "A ribald saga with supernatural underpinnings…Sharp production values… entertaining…with a jagged edginess that's rightening and riveting!"

Not bad for a first review that saw us at a disadvantage. Also, the poster painted by Dave Burke is great. Jana is now working full-time for *Lucinda's* and Randala is writing a script called *Phoenix Point,* to star myself

and Kelly (the girl next door). There have been a lot of
Phoenix Omens as a result.

3 July 1998

I talked with Colin Geddes from the Toronto Film
Festival today. He said that because I didn't actually
show Beatrice sucking the satyr's cock, the film probably doesn't cut it for the Midnight Movies section. He
also said it would probably be referred back to him if it
were submitted to any other section of the festival.
How's that for the criteria of the second most important film festival in the world?

Good news: The movie is complete and it looks gor-
geous on the big screen. I'm flying to Rome on Thursday
to submit the film to the Venice Film Fest. Also, I'm taking a fun series of ads out in *Variety* next week.

The first distributor to call us was Trimark, the company that, funnily enough, caused this film to be written.
Five years ago, they were looking for pitches for a se-
quel to the movie *Whore*, which starred Theresa Russell.
I wrote the synopsis for *Lucinda's Spell* in response, but
they turned it down.

And so *Lucinda's Spell* is completed and this book of
Omens comes to a close. A magical journey indeed, don't
you think?

From L to R: Director of photography Jaime Reynoso, myself, and Samantha Mehra. Samantha plays the truth sprite

The crew and cast of Lucinda's Spell *(I'm hugging Angie Green).*

Jana Pesek production designs the marketing for Lucinda's Spell. *Pink and black is our theme. She's a magical fairy. Can you tell? If you believe, she might sprinkle some of her fairy dust on you!*

Jason McHugh and I celebrate after the "Cannes You Dig It? Film Festival."

Top to bottom: Stephania Swinney, Kelly Williams, Betina and Jana Pesek. Heady days and nights promoting at the Venice (Italy) Film Festival.

Are you Elvis? Me now with my lovely family, Tina Leiu and our son Taliesin. Photo taken Halloween 2001.

"One of the most audacious indies released in recent memory, *Lucinda's Spell* demonstrates more creativity in a single reel than do most major studio films in their entirety. Jacobs has a unique vision and he puts it across with style and verve. This is one good-looking little picture. A lusty offbeat thoroughly delightful indie"
—*Video Business Weekly*

"Smart, Funny, Infectious. One of the most impressive independent films I've seen in a long time. Let it work its magic on you."
—**DVD review.COM**

"★ ★ ★! Fresh and Different. I recommend this movie to anyone interested in the Occult."
—*Fangoria*

"Way Cool! Fun, Irreverent and Eerie. Jon Jacobs is charismatic as hell!"
—*Cinescape*

"Incredibly bizarre, funny, perverse and more than a little absurd."
—*All Movie Guide*

"A fun eminently watchable film with real charm and heart"

—**FrightXmagazine.com**

"Charming!"

—**Amazon.com**

"A freakin' masterpiece"

—**Gamers Republic**

"If I didn't know any better I'd swear David Lynch directed this flick. It's Fun Odd and Entertaining, a great independent film"

—**Askew Reviews.com**

"★ ★ ★! A truly surprising find. One of the quirkiest films I've ever seen"

— *Jacksonville Film Journal*

"Energetic and entertaining. Fulton is a delight."

—**Film.com**

"Sexy, hip, violent and downright wacky!"

—*Videocy*

"An outrageous comedy about witches. A very funny, crazy movie! Jacobs does a fantastic job as Jason. Fulton is completely mesmerizing."

—**Videocrypt.com**

"I think Ken Russell and Fellini would have loved it!"

—**IMDB user reviews**

"Truly Something Special. Lucinda's Spell is Destined to become a Classic."
— ***Kaos 2000*** **magazine**

"Frenetic…looks and sounds great!"
—*New York Post*

"An enchanting version of modern day New Orleans"
—**Time Out! New York**

"Posh set design and fabulous costumes."
—*Village Voice*

"Breathtaking!"
—***Femme Fatales*** **magazine**

"A Bizarre, bawdy, black comedy."
—*New York Daily News*

"Christina Fulton has the quintessence, talent and gushing sex appeal to become a true luminary."
—**TheFilmSource.com**

"Jon Jacobs is destined for the big time. Miss it and you will miss out!"
— ***Phase9.net*** **magazine**

"Uninhibited and wildly misguided."
—*LA Weekly*

"Cocky but charismatic, giddy but genuine, everything about Jacobs brings *Trainspotting*'s sick boy to mind."
—***Freewheelin'*** **magazine**

"A perfectly directed fantasy of the Erotic kind."

—Emder zeitung

"Lucinda's spell demonstrates that great, colorful, fantastic independent films are possible."

—Northwest Net

"Frightening and riveting!"

—Variety

"A festival hit!"

—Film Echo

"Megacool!"

—Prinz

"Christina Fulton plays Lucinda with such unbridled fervor and warmth it leaves you speechless."

—Inside NWZ

"Sexy, fresh and fun, possesses a similar raw comedic energy to the Monty Python films with a bit of that Hong Kong action flair."

—World of Fandom

"A wonderfully offbeat, supernatural sex comedy with a lot of heart...outrageous sexuality and eye popping visual splendor"

—Margot Gerber, *American Cinemateque*

"A few more witches like Lucinda and the world would be saved!"

—Inside NWZ

1 June 2002,
Venice Beach, California

I am still working with many of the wonderful people I met during this period. I'm currently deeply involved in preparing to release on DVD through Golden Shadow Pictures all of the movies I did with Zero pictures as well as a new special edition of *Lucinda's Spell* and *The Girl With the Hungry Eyes*. It is my feeling this book will serve to shed some light on all these very special movies.

I watched *Harry Potter* on DVD yesterday. I was enthralled by the magic and I thought to myself—like so many other people—wouldn't it be great to live in a world like that? As I had that thought a little thrill ran up my spine as I realized that in publishing *The Book of Omens,* I am able to give back a little of the magic to the world that has been visited upon me.

As for the future…Well I'm still looking at the world in the same way, I'm still following the Omens and they have led me to the lovely Tina Leiu and to our magical son Taliesin. I'm also making a couple of new movies this summer: *Henry the Tenth* and *Hey, DJ.* The latter will star me, Tina Leiu, and my teenage pal Charlotte Lewis. Working with Charlotte is especially important because it brings another area of my life full circle and who knows? Maybe that's what we need to have ourselves a hit!

Finally I hope this book will inspire at least one person to recognize an important Omen in their life, that they may fulfill their dreams too.

Omen:

An occurrence or phenomenon believed to portend the future.

Johnny Famous
$19.95

Phoenix Point
$19.95

Dogstar
$19.95

The Wooden Gun
$19.95

Lucinda's Spell
$19.95

Mic and the Claw
$19.95

Prometheus Bound
$19.95

**The Girl with the
Hungry Eyes** $19.95

Vampires & Witches
$24.95

Welcome Says the Angel
$19.95

Hero, Lover, Fool
$19.95

T'ai Chi
$19.95

Buy these DVD's at amazon.com, ebay.com, rent at netflix.com, or send your order to Golden Shadow Pictures

Fax: 305-576-5943

Email: gsporders@hotmail.com

Or send a check to:
Golden Shadow Pictures
54 NE 43rd Street • Miami, FL 33137

(add $4.95 shipping per order)

Give the Gift of

The Book of
OMENS

to Your Friends and Colleagues

CHECK YOUR LEADING BOOKSTORE OR ORDER HERE

❑ **YES**, I want _______ copies of *The Book of Omens* at $19.95 each, plus $4.95 shipping per book (Florida residents please add $1.30 sales tax per book). Canadian orders must be accompanied by a postal money order in U.S. funds. Allow 15 days for delivery.

My check or money order for $___________ is enclosed.

Name ____

Organization ____

Address ____

City/State/Zip ____

Phone__________________________ E-mail __________________________

Please make your check payable and return to:

Spiral Staircase Publishing
54 N.E. 43rd Street
Miami, FL 33137